DIAMONDS
LIARS AND THIEVES

Wisdom Editions

Minneapolis

FIRST EDITION OCTOBER 2024

Diamonds – Liars and Thieves. Copyright © 2024 by Gia Nichols.
All rights reserved.

10 9 8 7 6 5 4 3 2 1
ISBN: 978-1-962834-28-5

Cover and interior design: Gary Lindberg

DIAMONDS
LIARS AND THIEVES

GIA NICHOLS

Wisdom
Editions
Minneapolis

Table of Contents

I would like to mention the following people who have made a significant contribution to my story and have stayed with me throughout this journey.

This includes Barbi Brookman who is no longer with us.

My husband Gregory.

Valerie J. Christell for her influence and creativity.

And Michael.

SGI U.S.A. for their hope and inspiration in my life.

I also dedicate this book to all the special people I have met and who work in retail. These wonderful people struggle daily in a very difficult industry. You are always remembered.

Episode 1:

Starting Over

How many people can say they have lived their entire lives in reverse? I married an alcoholic who happened to also be a drug addict. He was from a wealthy family. Unfortunately, addiction does not only affect the addict. For twenty-two years I lived with him and his extremes. Most of it was a life of tremendous abuse.

After leaving this horrible degrading mess, I started my life over at the age of 42 years old. I had no money, or job or prospects. All I had was a will to live, to become a success and therefore change my life.

It was a slightly overcast day. People were in a hurry rushing down the street. In both directions. What kind of a job could I do, I thought to myself. Walking down Michigan Ave in Chicago, I saw a sign in a window that caught my eye. It said Experienced Salesperson Wanted to Sell Beautiful Jewelry. I've always loved jewelry, and my mother had a beautiful collection. Putting on my best fake smile and taking a large gulp of air, I pushed open the heavy bronze doors to the store. I passed the security guards, and I asked to please see the manager. I glanced at my reflection in the full-length mirror. I think I looked attractive. I am petite. My blonde streaked hair fell gently down my back. My skin was slightly tanned, and I wore little makeup. My lips were full and the gloss that I had applied was just enough. The smokey eye makeup was an added accessory. I never left home without some sort of eye makeup. I'm of Mediterranean descent and my almond dark brown eyes needed a bit of accent. I thought I looked presentable. The suit I had chosen was chocolate brown and nipped in at my small waist. I finished it with three-inch heels. I don't want to look like a pipsqueak. Okay, I thought I am satisfied with how I look. I waited for the manager.

After about twenty minutes a tall man with a slight build appeared. His name was Mr. Edgar. He had blonde hair and spoke with a very heavy British accent. He seemed to be in his mid-thirties. He was dressed impeccably, in a tweed suit and tie. I thought he looked like a cliché. A Brit in tweed!

He had a very arrogant attitude and after several minutes of questions about my seemingly lack of experience, he arrogantly said, "Well I'm in a bit of a bind here. Usually I would say thanks but no experience, no job, but I lack sufficient help. I will give you an opportunity. You will have a chance for six weeks to show me you can sell and then we'll talk. I like your appearance." he said. "You look professional. You are an attractive lady. Maybe you might find a new life. I wish you luck. You will need it here."

I left the salon hopeful. This is indeed an opportunity, I told myself. Six weeks went by very quickly and I must say I met a lot of interesting people. They were kind and nasty. Some of the salespeople were out to get me. In spite of the negative, after six weeks no mention was made to me on whether I was staying or packing up.

I went to Mr. Edgar and cleared my throat. I said with a lightness in my voice, "Mr. Edgar, excuse me sir. You said you would give me six weeks and at the end of that time you would tell me whether you would keep me on or If I should gather my belongings and leave."

A strange smile came across his face. He rubbed his chin like Santa Claus. He said, "Why, Gia Nichols, would I sack the best salesperson who sells more than the other two stores combined." I knew a look of shock crossed my face because no one mentioned this to me!

I went home that night, but my feet never touched the pavement! I was very happy there for about a year.

Episode 2:

Work Continues

One summer day during that first year, a pretty young woman came into the store. She asked for Annie (one of the top salespeople). I was the only one on the floor and I knew the salesperson she was talking about was off that day. I explained the situation to her. I wished that I could have said you mean the trollop that throws herself at any man wearing a pair of pants!

The salesperson she was referring to was mid height with short blonde hair and big blue eyes. She was attractive. Okay she was very pretty. She was about 25 years old. If you want to say she was arrogant, she was very. If you want to say she was not a team player, okay. Let me just say she was a skinny bitch who thought she knew everything. She and I did not get along from the beginning. Actually, she didn't get along with anyone!

Anyway, this pretty young lady takes from her purse a long strand of Mikimoto Pearls. They were lovely and she slams them down on the case. "Tell her my husband knows I already have pearls from his mother!"

When she gave me her name, I knew that she was a wealthy well known woman whose husband was the son of a Congressional Senator. His uncle was a famous womanizer. It seems that genes spilled over to this generation as well. This kind of behavior happens quite often.

The next day when Annie came back, she laughed and for a second you would think we were friends. She told me the husband was trying to get her to deliver the pearls to his pied-`a-terre in the afternoon. This was probably the only civil conversation Annie, and I ever had because she was a jealous BITCH. She used to be First Sales Lady, until I came there. When I first started, everyone was helpful except her. She would give me wrong information and I learned right away to stay away from her. Something else bothered me too. I had heard her husband had a reputation as a thief. Several things had gone missing from our inventory. Now I was doubly concerned about this lying witch. The assistant manager also warned me to stay far away from her. It seems she was being watched.

The year flew by, and I was very happy. I continued to do well but stayed away from the BITCH. One day Mr. Edgar announced that he would be leaving and that he wished us all well. He then dropped the bomb that the owners of the stores were fighting. One brother had absconded with our beautiful color diamond collection. At that time it was worth several million dollars. The year was 1992. The collection was held in a giant motorized bee that would revolve and open and close. You would see every color of the rainbow in diamonds when it would open. It was the most magnificent display you would ever see! The bee was all white and black diamonds with yellow diamonds on its back. The colored diamonds inside the bee were small but beautiful.

We were told the store would go into liquidation and the salespeople would get wonderful commissions. In truth, the entire new group was as slippery as grease, but no one knew it. Annie was right in her element and became very good friends with the liquidators. I was told by the older salespeople exactly what kind of operation they were. Before they came, we were one of the best jewelry stores Chicago had to offer. After they left our reputation was not so good.

The liquidators also brought in some slimy salespeople that were as greasy as they were! They also interspersed their crap with our beautiful gems. Anyone with a trained eye could tell the difference. From the time I started working there, I studied everything I could! I learned a lot in one short year. Many times I was challenged by Annie (Bitch), but I always seemed to know the answer.

My gay friend Bob, who also worked there, helped me enormously. He told me never to let the bitch or any other salesperson intimidate me! He was a perfect friend! Even If you don't know the answer, give her attitude and she will back off! He was right MOST OF THE TIME.

We had every type of person visiting the store. Extremely rich, family rich, slippery rich mobsters, regular nice people, hookers and of course their "men." People in the entertainment industry were frequent visitors. Actually, just about every type of person you could think of came into the store, especially during the liquidation.

I made a big mistake recognizing an extremely rich acquaintance from my past life. I reminded him who I was. It was a big mistake! A salesperson only makes a comment if the customer recognizes her first!

Bob observed me and said, "Honey what were you trying to prove with that one? He's dating a slut! He left his wife for a piece of fine-looking ass, and he doesn't want anyone remembering him!"

I said to Bob, "If I do that again, slap me down will you?"

He laughed and said, "You're a baby. You will learn. Most of these people think we are one step up from shit anyway. Know your place and you will be fine!" I learned quickly, so the point was taken.

I also became friends with two older sales ladies. One lady, Yvette, was also a great help to me. She was petite and about fifteen years older than I was. She did not look her age and acted very youthful. She was knowledgeable. She was a big help! The other lady was Violet. She was older as well and we would speak French together. She mostly sold giftware. She was also slim as well and you instantly liked her. Our little group was wonderful, and we all got along well. As soon as the liquidators arrived, people started to look for other employment.

It was Christmas Eve, and I had experienced a piss poor couple of days. I was told this happens, however, when your rent is two months overdue and you are sneaking in and out of your Michigan Ave condominium because you can't pay the monthly assessment, you worry.

Annie said to me one cold, wet, miserable day, "Well, well, if it isn't our little star. How are YOU doing?"

I wouldn't give her any satisfaction, so I smiled and said, "Fine." This was the time we were working about twelve-hour days and besides being extremely tired, I was worried.

Episode 3:

Soka Gakkai Buddhism

About two weeks before this exchange with Annie, I met this wonderful lady, and she started talking to me about SGI Buddhism. She gave me books and magazines, and everything was so positive. I also knew it was the same religion my Idol Tina Turner studied. I thought if it helped her, maybe I can be helped as well. I began to chant. It was difficult at first but after a while it became easier. I needed to change my life and my luck. I would give it a try.

Soon I started to chant in the store under my breath. I didn't want anyone to think I was waiting for the little green men in white coats to come and get me. As it looked like I was talking to myself.

This Religion had a calming effect on me. I was Christened a Greek Orthodox Christian but was assured I could do both. I could make myself happy and others as well, simply by chanting. I thought if I can be happy and make others happy, I will give it a try!

11

Episode 4:

Santa Arrives

Now back to Christmas Eve. Out of nowhere, two used to be friends trotted into the showroom. One lady was at one time a good friend (I thought). Both were of Greek heritage. I happen to be first generation Greek as well, so we began conversing in Greek. I really wanted to disappear but oh well what's another slap.

"Honey," she exclaimed, that's the expression we Greeks use when we converse with one another. "How are you doing?"

"I'm fine," I said. "I'm a little tired but I'm okay."

With a snicker in her voice she cackled, "Oh you can handle it fine."

The other lady admonished her and said, "How dare you say that! Can't you see that the woman is tired? Really Betty you have no soul."

"Sorry, meant no harm." she retorted. "Anyway, we have to go shopping. Bye."

Bob observed this whole mess and said, "This was a friend?"

"Yes darling."

"You are much better off! Do you want to go home? I will cover for you."

"No," I said. I need to sell something, or I may start to eat the carpet in our living room."

"Why don't you and your kid come over for dinner at my house? If you can stand a few frustrated queens, it will be good food." I thanked him but went back to my post and stood there like a soldier.

It was fifteen minutes before closing. Everyone was rushing to get ready to leave. "Nam Myo Ho Renge Kyo," I chanted to myself tears began to well up.

A tall man dressed in shabby clean clothes, wearing a black leather jacket, came over to me and asked if I was busy?

"No sir, what can I help you with?"

"I'm not exactly sure but I was hoping you can guide me."

"I'm at your disposal sir."

"Thank you." he answered.

"What are dees green stones? Are they nice? Do ladies like them?"

"Yes sir, but they are a bit pricey. They are very fine Colombian emeralds. What were you interested in? Earrings, the ring, bracelet?"

He made a gesture with his hand like he was sweeping the floor. "All of them."

"All of the articles sir?"

"Ya."

"If you purchased all 3 pieces the price would be about $75,000, plus tax of course."

"Okay," He said," I'll take 'em! What are Dees red ones?"

"They are rubies sir." Mr. Dees Dems and Dose was very nice. I was thinking, is he for real?

"I like the ring, not sure she would like the other stuff."

"Okay, the ring is a Burmese ruby, so it is a bit costly."

"How costly?"

"It is $125,000." I answered back.

"It's a small red stone for so much money." he said.

"Can I show you something a little less expensive sir?"

"Naw, if she likes it she can have the other stuff too!" I think about this time I had my first hot flash, and I was only forty-two.

He hadn't asked me about any of the details associated with the pieces. The carat weight and provenance didn't seem to matter to him. I did not offer information, because he did not seem to care and was in a hurry.

"Anything else, I can show you sir?"

"Ya, I want two Rolex watches."

"Okay, what kind sir?" By this time Bob stopped what he was doing and came over to help me.

"One all yellow gold. I think it's called President something and the other is for my brother, a stainless-steel racing watch." Ka ching ka ching!

"Do you take credit cards mam?"

"Yes sir."

He handed me a Black American Express Credit Card. I tallied up the purchased items and gave him the total amount. "That is fine. Listen, I want to buy my girlfriend a ten-carat diamond ring. Can I come to see you next week?"

"Yes sir." I said.

Bob said under his breath, "A nice sale!"

My feet never touched the ground after that! I made a quick call to my son, Jim, anxious for him to answer. We are eating Christmas Eve dinner at the Drake Hotel tonight!

Episode 5:

Let's Count The Thieves

As usual, the day after Christmas there was a flurry of people coming and going! Some came to exchange, some returned and some to refund. Of course, my worst fear was that my Angel from Christmas Eve was going to return everything he bought. Good old Annie always checked the day's sales and when she saw mine, her eyes became as wide as saucers.

She marched over to me and smiled that obnoxious wait and see look. She said, "Well I see you had a nice sale. Who is he? Where did he come from?"

I said, "Last time I looked, I never had to answer to you." She smiled and walked away!

Bob, who was standing nearby, had watched her in action. He said, "You're learning to call her on everything. She is no one, especially to you!"

Unbeknownst to us both, she had made herself very useful to the slimeball liquidators and was doing everything she could to bury the original salespeople.

A few days later I heard from my angel client. He asked me to show him some diamond engagement rings. I was beyond happy. I went to the head liquidator and asked him to bring in some stones for me. He of course gave me the third degree. He asked me what the client did for a living. I simply said he wouldn't share his bank accounts with me, but from what I surmised, he was a Union Delegate. During the time of Richard J Daley that meant never ask. Mind your own business. He asked me for his phone number, which of course I was obliged to do.

Several weeks had passed and my favorite salesperson showed up with a full-length beaver coat, diamond studs and other goodies. Those of us who knew her knew she must be into some shady stuff.

Our assistant manager had confided in me before the store went into liquidation. She was being watched. "Stay away from her." she stated. "Two very expensive lapel clips from our Estate Collection disappeared. We suspect her." The assistant manager confirmed what I already suspected. It was a shame. Once the store went into liquidation she left. She knew the liquidators were slimy and she wanted no part of it.

Little Miss Thief was so full of herself on her last day. She announced she was going to a very special salon but would take some time off first! She was tired from working so hard! I bet she was tired! I began to really dislike her! I wondered what she or her thief husband were up to now. She was all wrapped up in her new beaver coat with a matching hat. Her diamond studs were of the best quality. I wondered where they came from.

A salesperson told me, "Gia Nichols, Mr. Webster wants to see you in his office." This comment interrupted my thoughts of the thief Annie.

I told Bob, "He probably got the diamonds in for my Mr. Rich!" I was very excited at the prospect of selling a ten plus carat diamond!

Actually, I got the size right on that, but this low life wanted me to know he was going to handle the sale himself, because he wanted a more experienced salesperson on it. Since Annie had left, he told me he was better qualified. I was pissed, hurt, angry.

I told Bob what had transpired. "Nichols, you better start paying attention around here. Keep a watchful eye on the inventory. We are selling a lot. Please notice how every day we are missing pieces. Be aware this is a slippery operation. Where do you think Annie got that beaver coat, diamond studs and enough money to stay home for a nice rest? Watch the salespeople these slime balls brought in. Don't be the last one to leave for your own good. Start looking for another job."

Things are not right! I'm such a naive person. I started thinking at that moment and after a few days I had it figured out. The people that were brought in were stealing with both hands. What was in the case in the morning was not necessarily there at night. There were missing receipts. When I questioned one man where were the diamond studs, he was doing inventory on?

He pointed to a tray. I asked where the 2.00ct diamond studs were? Also, where were the 1.50ct studs? He told me they were sent out for repair. Then he left. Three days later I asked him again and he said transferred out. Don't ask me any more questions. I'm not security.

My big diamond was sold to my Mr. Union Delegate. When I asked about the commission I was told, "Now you didn't sell the diamond, did you?" That was it for me. I started looking for another job.

I told Bob, "You are right. Bob there is so much crap going on, how could I not have known?"

"It's called education Nichols. What are you going to do?"

"I'm looking for another job."

He told me to check out a certain area. I was so grateful.

Episode 6:

Back To Square One – Discovering Where Things Disappeared into the Air

Pounding the pavement, I landed in the diamond center of Chicago. Talk about going from the best to sleazy. There I was. I made a mental note. I will keep at it and continue to learn and always go up in quality. Never do anything in a hurry and be the best I could be. I will also add that not all shops in the diamond district are sleazy.

I walked into a very bling, bling jewelry store. I did this because I noticed a sapphire ring that I LOVED from my fancy Michigan Ave store. It could have been a twin! I walked in and inquired about a sales position. Also, I mentioned where I had worked before. I said to the salesperson that a particular ring caught my eye. I might be interested, as I had a boyfriend who liked to buy me nice things. In truth, there was no one but I wanted to know about that ring! Where did it come from?

A short stocky man appeared. He said he was the owner and was I interested in a job? "Oh yes!" I exclaimed and though I had worked on Michigan Ave I would not mind in the least to travel to such a fine establishment. In reality, I was of course lying through my teeth I then asked about the blue sapphire in the case.

"Oh, the sapphire ring is from Ceylon. Someone who works for the company is able to find us only the BEST they have to sell."

"Really?" I said.

"Yes, maybe you would like to see other gems from this fine establishment? It's a shame they are going broke. I was lucky to know this person and make the connection."

"I might like to look at other gemstones." I said.

"It would be my pleasure," he said. Out came some diamond papers and low and behold two mounted stones I recognized right away.

"You have a very good eye," my pudgy friend exclaimed.

"How did you know these came from the same lot?"

All of a sudden, the light of money went out in his eyes. He gathered up his merchandise and said, "I think we are finished here. I have an urgent call I'm expected to make. Let me know if you need a job and we will discuss your options, bye."

Well I had the inside track, and she was indeed fencing her loot. I can't understand why she would sell a mounted ring. Even though it was beautiful, it screams HOT!

Bob said to me, "She was getting careless and her husband for certain is a thief and could care less! What do we do now?"

"Bob, the evidence is right in front of us."

"I will go with Susan," he said, "and have a peek but aside from that, she is scot-free!"

A week later he went with one of our sales ladies and I was 100 percent right. If we were dealing with a regular store, things would be different. Slime always stays with the same element. Funny how needing to put food on your table and pay bills makes you forget about thieves you unfortunately know!

A New Position

A couple of weeks later I found a job in the diamond district. It wasn't sleazy in the first place, but it definitely was of questionable reputation.

The boss was a very sexy handsome kind of guy. He knew it too! He flirted with anyone that walked into his office who was remotely attractive. Of course, he was a happily married man. Monday through Friday he was in Chicago at work. Friday through Sunday he went home to the little woman and the three kids out of state, of course.

Bob and I started to take Country Western dancing. It was a lot of fun! He also joined the jewelry shop where I was employed. As did a few more reputable salespeople from the previous salon. I met a new salesperson. He was a doll named Alan. He was so sweet and really fit into our group. The good news was, there was no Annie!

Country Western music and dancing was very popular at the time and there were quite a few bars in Lincoln Park. I had never done this kind of dancing. I was a great dancer. I thought it would be fun to give it a try. I am a fast learner. Spending time with gay men at Country Western bars was a real hoot! We learned to dance! It was safe, non-threatening and the boys were so much fun. We were like girlfriends having a good time!

During the down time at work and in the jewelry business, there is a lot of down time, we talked about the nightly activities and who was going to join us. One night the boys decided we had been going to straight bars too often and wanted some of their own action!

I said, "Fine but what am I going to do?"

They said, "You will dance and have fun and just not only be with men."

"Okay." I said. They had always been so generous with me going to straight country bars, count me in. I could always trust my friends to look out for me.

Both guys were good looking and tall. They were very fit gay men. They kept their bodies in tip top shape. Both were super fit! Also, they were great dancers! Walking into this bar was like walking into a gorgeous gym! Every man was as fit as could be, and all were gay. How safe and disappointed could one woman be!

From over my shoulder came a voice that was definitely female. She was about the same height as I was. I am 5'2" and 99 lbs. and not that it mattered but it was the time of the mini dress. It was my dress of choice since I was so petite. My hair was two tone blonde, to my shoulders and if I do say so I was very pretty. Being pretty did not matter here. She was slightly masculine and a nice-looking black lady.

"Dance?" she asked.

"Sure." I said back.

"Do you lead or follow?"

"Oh I could go either way."

Wrong thing to say, she had this smile on her lips that looked like a perfect answer! I was wrong! She turned out to be a very nice lady. Who by the way, was a good dancer! After a few dances she wanted to get cozy. I had to explain the situation to her. After that little discussion it was au revoir!

A couple hours later, I was tired and wanted to go home. I said to my friends, "I'm out of here. See you all at work tomorrow, be safe!" It was the time of Aids, and though I knew Bob was safe, Alan was not. Even though I worried, it was not my business. So home I went, alone.

Episode 8:

Getting too Cozy.
Work Continues

The next day at work both guys were hung over and wanted no more dance clubs. My handsome boss took note of our conversations and asked if he could join the group the next time we went to a straight bar.

I answered back to him, "What about your wife?"

"She will not be joining us." He flippantly shot back. It is great exercise. He told me she wanted him to be with our group and enjoy himself, because she realized how very lonely he was.

At first, I believed his story. Bob, my friend, and Alan, my other friend, told me to be aware that my boss had the hots for me. It was very evident according to my friends. This was the 90's and sexual harassment wasn't really out in the open or discussed at that time. Naive me, thought he was being nice. He was just lonely and liked dancing. He wanted to be a part of our small group. He started making little jokes, complimenting me and wherever I was in the salon, he was next to me. Finally, one night while we were dancing the Stationary Cha-Cha, he got too close. I tried to toss it off, but I felt uncomfortable.

Bob said I was in for it now. "What are you going to do when he makes the big play?"

I said, "He's married!"

"So what?" they both answered. "He has you here and her there. It is perfect!"

It was a Tuesday night and Pat announced he was going to join the group and practice his Double Two Steps.

Previously a man stopped into the store before closing, and I recognized him as a customer I had worked with. I had sold him a very high-end diamond wedding band for an upcoming anniversary a few weeks back. He brought out the wedding band and it was all mangled. Diamonds were missing and the metal, 18Kt white gold, was all scratched and destroyed.

I said, "It looks like it fell down a garbage disposal!"

He snapped at me. "We have a live-in maid. My wife pushes paper at her job. How dare you infer this to me!"

Out of nowhere, my boss was next to me. He took the man into his office and before I knew what happened, the two were laughing and best friends. Pat said, "We will take care of it. You will not be responsible for the repair." I was shocked at the change in him!

My boss said to me, "You owe me big time!"

I retorted back. "It was clear what happened."

Pat said, "Sometimes you have to let the client think he got the best of us. Kissing ass happens. Now you owe me a BIG FAVOR! Nichols, I plan on collecting too!"

"What are you talking about?" I innocently replied.

"I took care of this creep for you and now we will go to the Country dance bar and have fun!"

I told Bob and Alan the whole story. They had warned me this was going to happen. I hate that I told you so! He was making moves on me the entire night! As I said he was extremely handsome. Tall, dark and gorgeous. He had jet black hair. Dark blue eyes. The longest lashes I had ever seen. He was show stopping to any woman or man.

He had a drinking problem. He loved beer, vodka martinis and scotch. He probably would drink grain alcohol. He was very bright. He was also well read and could talk on any subject. In short, he could charm you in any direction he wanted to go. I liked good looking guys. If a man was bright, as well as tall and handsome that's it. I'm attracted!

He was about seven years younger than me. We looked the same age. He was 36, and I was 43. He always paid me compliments. Which of course any woman would love. He was very lonely. That was obvious! The gay guys would joke that if he ever went gay, they would all be in line fighting over him!

Believe me, he was one hundred percent man! It was getting difficult to avoid him at work. He stalked me like a lion stalks its prey. The sales associates would all make jokes and bets as to who would weaken first! What they didn't know was that I came from a very strict old fashioned Greek family, and I had been raised with very tight morals. The fight inside myself was very great.

Also, It did not help that I was very lonely! My hormones were working overtime and his were triple mine for sure! This continued to be a cat and mouse game. Some of us had decided to visit our favorite bar and do some dancing. My boss, always within earshot of me, invited himself along. That night I was wearing a red ultra suede mini dress with high heels and the dress had buttons down the back to a slit that was quite sexy for the time. Here we were a magnificent group of after-hours jewelers going out for some clean wholesome fun! I might add that one of the other girls who was a graduate gemologist wanted to join us. In total we were a group of seven.

Episode 9:

A Big Mistake, Almost

It was about 4:30pm and we were thinking about the night's activities when a client strolled into the salon. He was looking to sell a diamond ring and wanted to know if we had any interest. My boss was tied up with another client, so he handed the prospect to Susan, the gemologist. She looked at the ring and after some calculations declared it to be about a 5ct emerald cut F VS2. The second in charge was busy so no one else could verify her evaluation. Knowing Susan was a competent gemologist they decided to make the deal. She gets a check issued to the client. He was anxious to leave, and we were anxious for the night's activities.

My boss comes strolling through the showroom and asked Susan, "What's going on?" She tells him about the stone and the money we were going to make. He said, "Let me have a look."

It turned out to be Moissanite. Which is a simulated type of stone that is difficult to distinguish from an authentic diamond. He caught it though! The man almost made it to the elevator and Susan almost lost her job! Of course, it helped that she was the owner's niece, lucky her. Anyone else would have been out the door. Lucky us, because it would have ruined everyone's evening! You can bet that never happened again.

That night we all had plenty to drink. What a close call that was! Not to be funny but nepotism goes a long way. The owner was a rich man and hardly ever visited the salon. He relied on Pat. A big catastrophe was averted!

We were all feeling pretty good after that almost disastrous incident! The music started to play, and I didn't stop dancing for a minute. Finally, my boss got really pissed and made a comment.

I told Pat, "It's after work and I do not have to answer to anyone."

He gave me the saddest look and said "Please, I need to dance with you."

Bob was watching the exchange and said to me, "You better dance with him. He's not too happy and we will have to bear the brunt of his wrath, because you refused to dance with him."

The music started and I turned to him and said "Ok." You would think I gave him a million dollars!

Did he hold me too close? You bet he did. It was difficult to breathe because he held me so tight. Besides knowing how inappropriate it was, I had to see the sales force watching us. I reminded Pat he was a married man. This does not happen in my world! He quickly broke his embrace, knocked down a shot and took a taxi home to his rented apartment.

The next day he called me into his office and gave me a talking to that would make you red in the face. "I just wanted to dance with you. That's it!"

"Listen," I spoke up, "you and I know that is a BS statement! You know that you are very interested in me. Don't deny it. Everyone notices the electricity between us, and it stops now."

He told me to close the door, and I obeyed. He said, "Look It's obvious I'm crazy for you. However knowing you, I understand it could never be anything. I'm here Monday through Friday, you all go dancing. Please let me be part of the group."

"That is NOT professional!" I shot back. "You are employing us to work. After that, It's our own time."

He pleaded, "Just let me be a part of the group. I promise to behave with you!"

Famous last words! I thought.

"You will see. I will not touch you."

After a long discussion with Alan and Bob we decided we would have no peace if we didn't include Pat. Damn, why did he have to be married? Why was he so damn intelligent? Most important, why was he so fucking handsome? I know this was going to be testing my moral character. I was not happy.

He continued following me at work. The cat and mouse game continued on as well. How we ever got work done is beyond me. At night it was non-stop dancing and drinking. Not me, because I did not drink very much. Everyone else drank to excess.

One night it was pouring rain, and everyone piled into two cabs to go home. Susan pulled me aside and we had a one-sided discussion. "I know Pat's family and they are so wonderful. I know what he's trying to do, and you better stop it. Not only will you destroy yourself, but things will not go well around here!"

I told Pat the story. "He said listen, all will work out. I promise."

Sure, sure I thought. A man with a throbbing Dick knows he can work it out. I, of course, knew better!

How did business go? Well, we sold so much that Christmas, it was ridiculous.

The owner pulled me aside and said, "I've seen nothing, but good things happen because of your work around here."

He wasn't talking about the night dancing. I was working and selling like no one else. Pat noticed my progress and of course, I got a raise. The figures spoke for themselves, and I outsold everyone!

The cat and mouse game still continued. One night we were doing the stationary Cha-cha. The electricity as usual between us was unbelievable. He dipped his body towards mine and held me so close I could barely breathe. After he spun me around back, I was so close to him. I was almost standing in back of him. I cannot go on like this I thought. He had a tremendous erection. I could feel it because we were so close. I told Alan, my other friend who I worked with, the story. Of course, he almost knew everything because of Bob.

"Why don't you just screw him and be done with it?"

I said, "It might be my ego, but he will never leave me alone for sure! Besides, my mother gave me morals and I won't sleep with a married man."

"So don't sleep with him! Screw him and then throw him out."

"Oh Alan, I still remember how cute and sweet you were. No, my sense of what's right and what's wrong will not allow me to do this."

"You will be miserable if you don't. Have a quick roll in the hay. Frankly, my dear, it wouldn't hurt you either. We can all see it is not a one-sided deal." Alan was always so intuitive.

Episode 10:

Let's Try Something New

"I know what we should do tonight!" Alan announced. "Let's go to the Excalibur Nightclub. We let them go to the Whiskey Dance club and we will have our own fun."

"It's a straight club." I said to him.

"So what?" he shot back. "I can have fun dancing with women too."

"Okay," I said, "that would be a good change!"

Before I knew it the Gemologist Sue invited herself with us and off the three of us went. Bob and Pat went to the Whiskey and Alan, Sue and I went to Excalibur to dance Disco. That was quite popular at the time, as well. We had so much fun! I didn't have to think about Pat's mooning eyes undressing me. It was a non-threatening environment.

After about two hours I had danced my butt off and was tired and ready to go home. I don't remember when Sue left. Leave it to Alan, he found a gay group and was having the time of his life. I was about to take a taxi home. I felt someone staring at me. I turned around and there was a very handsome, very young man. He was at least 10 years younger than me. I was forty-four. He had to be in his late twenties or early thirties.

I told Alan and he said, "That guy has been staring at you all night. I thought he was looking at me when we walked in, but it was you."

I answered back, "How do you know this?"

"I know because I asked him if he wanted to hang out with me. He said he was interested in my friend and were we together? I told him I was gay, but you were available."

After about twenty minutes or so, I had enough. He wouldn't stop staring at me. I walked up to him and said, "You have been watching me all night. Either ask me to dance or quit staring."

He smiled and said with a thick middle Eastern accent, "Would you dance with me please?"

"Sure," I said, "let's go." He was a great dancer and could slow dance! His name was Michael, and he was an attorney for the Israeli Government. He came to Chicago on business every month.

He asked to see me again. I said, "I do not know you."

He retorted, "I will give you the number of my office and they will vouch for me."

"In Israel?" I asked.

"Either there or here." he said.

By the way, he was thirty-three years old. I told him I was more than ten years older than him and to find someone his own age.

He looked straight through me and remarked. "You look younger than me so who cares?"

I laughed! I guess I did look pretty young. Ego sometimes can be a good thing.

I said, "I would think about it." I gave him my number at work. I just wanted to be safe. The next day Alan couldn't wait to tell everyone about my guy. Pat heard about it and questioned me, and then had an attitude all day long.

"You ditched me last night." he complained.

"I didn't know we were a couple?" I shot back. "I decided I would go with Alan somewhere new. It is none of your business." Pissed off, he turned and walked away with an attitude.

I heard from Michael at about 1;00pm and of course he asked me if I called his office? He had given me his business card.

"No." I said.

He then retorted, "Why not? I have very excellent credentials. Call my office in Tel Aviv and they will tell you about me."

"No, forget it."

"What can I say to please get you to go out with me for dinner?"

"You are too young for me." I said.

He looked at me and actually had the nerve to say. "Is it because I'm Jewish?"

I got really pissed with that statement. "I don't care what your ethnicity or religious beliefs are. You are too young."

"It's just dinner. I have a request to ask of you."

"Sure." I did not say I would go with him.

"If you go with me, we have to go to a Kosher restaurant because I'm Orthodox." I looked at him and not wanting him to think I was Anti-Semitic I agreed. I didn't know what an orthodox person was. "I will pick you up wherever you like."

"Okay, pick me up at work about 6:00pm."

"Fine!" he said, overjoyed. You would think I gave him a million dollars.!

At 6:00PM sharp, he came to the store. Three women approached him and were foaming at the mouth. He was darling with an adorable sense of humor. Pat, of course noticed, and his deep blue eyes turned green with envy.

Episode 11:

Just A Date?
The Showdown

Out we went. I was wearing my tight black dress showing a slight bit of cleavage. He immediately told me I was the most gorgeous girl he had ever seen. He was dressed in a suit and tie and looked very handsome. He was not as tall as Pat, but he was very bright and that made up for the height. The food was great. We danced and he was a gentleman. His personality was amazing, and his accent was sexy! We took a taxi to my apartment and at the door he pulled me to him and gave me a beautiful kiss.

"Look," he said, "I'm really interested in you. Please see me again. In fact, I travel a lot. Would you go with me on trips?"

"Hold on, you don't even know me."

"That will change," he said.

"Pretty sure of yourself aren't you."

He then pulled out his briefcase and gave me his picture and his huge resumé of his work. "We were made for each other."

"Look," I said, "I'm Greek Orthodox, and you are Jewish don't you care?"

"No, do you?"

"No." I said.

He told me that in two hours he knew we were made for each other. "I'm leaving tomorrow and will be back in two weeks. We will spend every free moment together." He kissed me again and I was a little light-headed. "Goodnight my Gia and I will call you when I get back to my hotel."

He called me that night and we were on the phone for an hour or more. The next day he called me at work and though I couldn't speak for long it was wonderful!

His resumé was incredible! He was an attorney for the Israeli Government. He had so many credentials. Many people held his position in very high esteem. He had wonderful commendations from the highest government officials in the United States offices where he worked.

Pat was furious but tried to hide it. The next night he asked to go to the Whiskey to dance. I did not want to go and made a very feeble excuse.

"Oh you only go out with Israeli government guys?"

"No, I only go out with unmarried men."

Pissed off he turned and walked away. Yay I thought, I'm finally through with him.

At 6:00pm Alan says to me, "We are all going to the Whiskey, and you are, too."

"No!" I retorted. "I can't take anymore of Pat's crap. I'm not interested. Sue thinks I'm going to wreck his marriage, and I don't want the drama of a married man!"

"Gia, you know he will make it impossible for the rest of us if you are not with us."

Well dear reader, you know I gave in and went along. Great dancing and yes, he was the sexiest man. I don't want to start up with this shit! It will destroy me and I'm not going to destroy his marriage. Bottom line, he took me home and we kissed. If he wasn't married that would have been it! Little Miss Moral Majority. I told him that's it! I'm quitting and it's over before it starts. These were the days before sexual harassment as I had mentioned before. There was no way out for me.

"Do you have another job?" he asked. My friends asked the same thing.

"Nope but I will find one! I'm done with this tight-rope act. Your kisses are like drugs that I have to have."

"Gia, we were made for each other." as he continued on with deep kisses. His hands started moving over my body. He pressed his lower part of his body against me, and my breath caught in my throat. "Let me come in for a few minutes and I know I can make you so happy. I am crazy about you Gia. We belong together. If you don't let me make love to you, I will go crazy."

I don't know how I did it, but I pushed him away.

"He came back for more. Let me come in just for a little while. I can make you happy baby."

Really Pat? While we are making each other happy, we will know your wife is married to a cheater and I will be a whore."

"I will leave her!"

"No!" I shot back sharply. "You will leave me right here and take your hard-on home to your wife." That gorgeous man haunted me for a long time. The next day I decided I would leave this place.

No one walks out without having another job lined up, my coworkers all chimed in. While working at my current job I continued my Buddhist studies practicing Nam Myo Ho Renge Kyo. My sales had improved greatly. In fact, more than I could have imagined. I loved the Buddhist meetings, and the people were the kindest, I had ever met. They offered encouragement with every situation. They were so happy that I thought they were all on some kind of happy pills.

I must tell you this was the reason that pushed me to change my job. I couldn't stand Pat's moaning and the pressure from all his drama. I was crazy about him and on the brink of having him in my bed. I wanted him so badly. However, I knew in the end it would destroy me. Also, I had taken over other jobs within the company. I was refused a raise because the owner was the cheapest man I had ever met.

I chanted for great change and happiness and took a leap of faith.

Back to the Other Side of Town

I had a friend who worked on Michigan Ave at a very chic jewelry store. I interviewed and was hired immediately. It was a store that was French owned. It was not a forever job, and I knew it. It was a job to tide me over until I had the opportunity to find a salon that was only jewelry. This salon was known for its handbags and clothes as well as faux jewelry.

There was plenty of drama there but a different kind. It was commission sales so there was pressure to sell as much as you can. There was added pressure because it was a new department, and they had to prove their worth.

Clothes and accessories sold quickly. Faux, or fake jewelry, also sold in great numbers. No one had ever heard of fine jewelry being sold there. We were like prospectors. We had to educate the public. Sell not only the jewelry but sell the famous story. We had to romance the product! I got the hang of it. Every event that was held in the evening would find me telling the story of how the Fine Jewelry Salon came to exist. I became very good at it. I always excelled at public speaking. Having been a singer, I loved being in front of people. Never ever was there a bit of nervousness in any of my presentations.

My boss had me try and train the other two girls. They did not have my personality. They were fine but I had animation. I made the story exciting and seemingly come to life. I loved the evening events. Imagine you are transported back to 1910. I started from the beginning and ended up in fine Jewelry 1932. It was very glamorous and filled with intrigue. Clients were mesmerized and wanted to know as much as I would tell them.

One night the owner of my previous job visited with his wife. They hardly ever visited Chicago. Pat took care of everything. There was no need for him to visit, as long as the money kept pouring in. He listened to my presentation. I did not see him or his wife, until he presented himself to me.

He said, "You are a credit to the store!" He enjoyed the background story. "Learn as much as you can," he announced. "I just bought the old salon you began in. I'm going to make it as elegant as it once was. I will need someone to handle business and to promote the name that was once so fantastic. It is now a mess, but we can resurrect everything! Do you think you would like to work for me again?"

I wanted to ask whether Pat will be a part of this new offer? I smiled coyly and replied, "You never know." But I knew, never in a million years!

Welcome to C&F
or Welcome to Hell

The opportunity presented itself for a high-end jewelry only store. My friend Yvette told me they were looking for a talented salesperson and she thought of me. Pressure and greed. The wealthiest people visited this establishment. It had the most beautiful jewelry I've ever seen.

Now let me tell you about drama. This is where Diamonds Liars and Thieves really starts. The beginning of my story was an appetizer. Of course, I will start with the most incredible inventory you would have ever seen at that time. Let me start at the beginning.

An immense gold opulent door so very impressive and foreboding led you inside. There were gold bars on the doors and on the outside display windows. It was the most elegant look I've ever seen on the Magnificent Mile! It made my first job look like a bargain basement set-up.

You entered and were buzzed in through this gorgeous door. Then you noticed the sales floor was divided into sections. At the very front sat off duty police officers. They were armed, well dressed and looking dangerous. My last job in the diamond district, had an elderly security man who usually fell asleep in the corner while on duty. Lucky for us we had very few incidents.

This definitely was different! The salespeople sat scattered at desks that were placed along elegant and large walls. Display cases were placed all around the large entry walls and above the desks so the salespeople could open and show off the delectable goodies! A huge display case was in the middle of the store and many of the finest watches were displayed in this case. The side cases had rings with semi-precious stones. Diamond earrings and necklaces, everything was of the very finest quality. It was like being in a candy store. Only this candy was jewelry. You didn't know where to look because there was so much inventory.

I told myself as I entered do not act like a hick. I have seen beautiful things like this before, just not so much. It was similar to the very first job I had but on a smaller scale with much more high-end jewels exhibited. I composed myself and stood ready for the interview. I was shown into an office in the back of the main showroom. There were about five other offices and a very large office right off the main floor.

I caught a glimpse of myself. Not bad I thought my honey blonde streaked hair was up in a French twist with messy tendrils on the side. I was dressed in black. It was not only my favorite color but for a diamond sales-person, it was the best for showing off the inventory. My make up was minimal with the eye make up being the key. Smokey eyes with dark eyeliner. High heels and a very tight tailored skirt. I had learned a lot from my pre-vious work experiences. My tight black Jacket finished off the look and showed my curvaceous body to its best advantage, while really down playing the sexy image. I looked elegant and sophisticated. This was the look of most of the ladies that worked there and something I had learned from my previous jobs. Look elegant but you are not the focus, the diamonds are!

While waiting for my interview I noticed the many security cameras placed in all the strategic ar-eas. I felt like I was in Fort Knox. So, there I sat waiting for my interview. After about fifteen minutes or so, an elderly paunchy man with graying hair came into the office and introduced himself as the owner of the store. He had the worst breath I had ever en-countered! His name was Bernard Stein. He spit as he talked. It was not pleasant, but I guess there are far worse things. He took my resumé. Glancing at it, he told me we had a very special clientele. It would take me a while to get used to the unique way he did business. He wasn't kidding, that was for sure!

He said he had heard about me from my friend and that he liked the way I sounded. He also mentioned it was a straight salary job and as I show productivity, I will have my pay increased. I wasn't keen about that because commission sales are what you want. He said he liked straight salary, because then there was no competition between salespeople. Also, he warned me about talking about salary with the other salespeople. He didn't like dissention of any kind. He told me he treated everyone the same and that is one of the main reasons. He didn't want people discussing their pay.

I learned he was a suave liar and played favorites. He was very cheap and wanted as much from the working staff as he could get. He would not have you discuss salary because he played favorites. A few women and men did ten percent work but were paid so much more, because they were his favorites. That is how I came to The Golden Door of Elegant Jewels.

Episode 14:

Exploring the Salon and Employees

He told me one of the other sales associates would give me a guided tour and explain the setup and the system in place. The next day I showed up promptly at eight thirty am and was shown around the Shit Show. That is what it was, gentle reader. Stay tuned for the many reasons why.

Not to get off track, let's resume the tour. There was a hallway that passed you from front to the back. That way you could enter the back offices. In the back you saw a loft-like room connected to another smaller room that housed three huge safes. In the main office sat Bernard Stein and his group of merry lunatics.

The manager was an overweight woman slightly older than me with a paunchy stomach and a swollen face. This was either from too much booze, food or both. She was very cold looking. I soon learned she had an ego problem. She acted like her shit didn't stink. She thought she knew everything. Her hair was very dark. It looked like a bad dye job. It was styled a couple of inches below her ears. I wouldn't exactly call her stylish, more like frumpy. She was Mr. Stein's right hand as he referred to her. Her name was Julie Coyle. Personally, after a week my opinion was, she couldn't find her way out of a paper bag with directions on it! I know I'm on the light side of being critical. You could also tell at one time she was pretty. If this place drives you to look like this I thought, I don't think I will be here long!

Next to her sat a computer Geek. David Stubl, who didn't know much about computers but pretended he did. He lived way above his means and was overpaid because he was Mr. Stein's friend. Next to him sat the inventory controller Myron Garrick. He was another middle-aged man who kissed Mr. Stein's Golden ass. He spoke very little, usually just sarcastic comments.

Lastly, sat Mr. Stein's trusted secretary who wrote his correspondence and was a Bahamian import. She worked for him for about 20 years. She didn't say much but again had a heavy dose of sarcasm in her demeanor. Above their heads, there were security monitors showing the entrance, the main floor and all the offices. Occasionally, the monitor would jump to the upstairs loft where three more people sat. You could go upstairs via the stairs in the back or go via the stairs in the front. As you entered the building you could not see the stairs in the front.

There was a door that closed off this area. Opposite the stairs was an elevator that went to the second and third floors. You needed a key to access it. The loft in the back was quite large and upstairs there were another two safes. There were cabinets holding appraisals and more information on various vendors and appraisals of clients purchases. They were in a bygone era, still doing things on paper. Not too much computer work was ever done.

At the back of the loft sat the most knowledgeable man in the entire salon, Joseph Brickmann. He was a graduate gemologist, horological wizard and a very savvy salesman! He knew pretty much everything there was to know about diamonds, gemstones, watches and anything else pertaining to jewelry. In general, he did the work of three people. He was tall and slender with graying hair. He ate only vegetarian food and was always at his desk. Usually, it was peanut butter and jelly or a cheese sandwich. Mr. Stein depended on his expertise and worked him like a mule. He wasn't one of his treasured kiss- ass people so he was underpaid and overworked.

Next to Joseph, sat Rosa. She was a medium sized lady of Mexican descent. She had dark black hair. She loved to tell stories about her old, haunted house. There were always stories about her family. She was very kind and interesting. She logged and tagged every item that came into the salon.

Next to her sat the shipper who sent items out to clients and vendors. He also accepted packages. He was from India and his name was very long, so we just called him Jax. He was a hoot. Half his day was spent shipping. The rest of the time he was looking at porn on his computer and talking about anything and everyone. He knew the sales associates and he also knew what everyone's salary was. I guess you could call him a busy body, but he was likable for the most part. You could see he was treated pretty low on the totem pole. He would curse the management team under his breath. To the salespeople, in general, he was nice.

In the back of the loft sat Vasha, the bookkeeper. She immigrated from Poland. She had a thick accent. She did her work, and you never saw too much of her. She was sarcastic like the rest of the chosen few. She loved to use adjectives like sweetie and darling girl. She also loved to show her worth whenever possible. Generally, she could annoy the shit out of you. I found the less I had to do with her the better off I was. She turned her accent off and on at will. It could piss you off at how much she pretended to know. She wasn't stupid but she wasn't brilliant either.

Two steps up from the loft was the kitchen where you could have your lunch and take a break. Breaks were few and far between. The monitors were on and always kept track of where the employees were. I was glad they didn't have a monitor in the restrooms, or we would have had nowhere to go. In the back of the lunchroom was Mr. Stein's private offices. There were no monitors there. You never went back there unless you wanted to use the front stairs to go down to the floor or access the window displays. It was interesting that the monitors were supposed to have film in them, but they didn't. We will get into that later.

This was the set up. Welcome to Cooper and Flux. I have no idea how the name came to be.

In the ten years that I was there we had the wealthiest people from not only Chicago but worldwide! Of course you couldn't talk about who visited. The only time I will give an actual name because they are now deceased. There were about ten sales associates at any given time at the salon and Bernard wanted his pound of flesh from all of them!

I had been there a short time, when Bernard and Mrs. Stein went to Switzerland to buy watches and other fancy specialty items. Of course, they took the manager, Julie Coyle, with them. She went everywhere they did. We thought that years ago Mr. Stein had an affair with her and now Mrs. Stein goes with them to buy. Julie pretends she knows what she's looking at and Mrs. Stein goes to shop for herself. She had at least one of everything in her possession. If she didn't have a particular item, she would come into the store and go into the main vault. She would shop to wear something special to show off to her wealthy society friends. She would go out to lunch, dinner or some event. She always helped herself.

Mr. Stein would say, "Oh Sylvia don't take that, it is new. I need to sell it and make some money." She would take it anyway because she always got whatever she wanted.

Sylvia Stein was a very chic looking older woman with gray hair and a good figure. She always knew how to fix herself up elegantly. I don't understand how she could stand his breath. Since he was well worth over one hundred million dollars, I guess she bought him mints! They seemed like they had genuine affection for each other. Every once and a while he would pat her backside. By the same token if she ever caught him do-ing anything she would fix him good! She apparently taught her daughter her tricks because she also married very well.

Off they all went to Switzerland to buy for the store, and you would think the inmates were on holiday! There was no screaming in the back offices. We did our work but there was no tension. To say Bernard Stein and Julie caused tension is an understatement.!

Anyway, I'm on the floor still learning the ins and outs of the salon. I was productive but not a shining star. I was reminded there was no commission so just do your best work. I was also told jokingly, don't try to jump over the desk to get to another customer because it doesn't matter.

Episode 15:

Barbi Brookman

One day I'm sitting at a desk and a fifty something pretty woman walks in. She was dressed in tight jeans. She was tall with a very nice tan. Her honey blonde hair cascaded to just below her shoulders. She was wearing high heels and the blouse she wore revealed amazing assets.

As she looked around, I noticed all the sales associates were sitting down. No one got up to approach her. Most of the people had been with Mr. Stein a long time, so they knew a lot of his clients. This woman was apparently not known. Not one associate was going to bust their ass for her. I was sitting at the desk chanting to myself observing the lack of interest. I thought, well I don't care if she can afford anything. This is not right. I got up and greeted her.

Her name was Barbi Brookman. She was very friendly and had a quirky personality. She looked at a lot of very expensive high-end pieces. We hit it off very well. I spent about an hour with her.

One of the older ladies said to me, "Why are you wasting your time with that one? She is a cheap chicken." I didn't know what that meant so I looked quizzically at her. "Oh she comes in here all the time but rarely buys."

I didn't care. "I have nothing else to do and she seems nice."

The older lady sighed and said, "You will learn."

I thought to myself, you never know who is buying. I remembered my Christmas sale at my first job and knew to never judge a book by its cover. I'm sure she knew that too. However, since the old man wasn't there, she wasn't going to move herself for anyone. Anyway, Barbi confided in me that she was on a dating site and had met someone who promised to buy her a lot of nice things. It sounded like famous last words. Again, you never know.

This was the way it worked at Cooper and Flux or C&F as we referred to it. Do not confuse it with Cutthroat and Fuck. (LOL) The retail price was listed on the tag. We would get you a special price from the boss! Of course the boss wasn't there. In his absence we would go to the cold bitch Julie. In this instance she wasn't there either. Next in charge was Joseph Brickmann.

Every time you would walk in the back for a price the drill was the same. "WHO IS THIS PERSON? Is she a known customer? Is she in society? Is she an entertainer from Hollywood? We did a lot of business with these people. Does she have any money? Do you know her?"

This was the drill with every price that was ever given. It got to be so trite and awful that sometimes you would make something up. If you were a known person, you got the best price. This woman didn't stand a chance. I got ticked off by the snide remarks everyone in the back always made. I was new at this time and hadn't learned how nasty they could all be. As well as sarcastic and down-right horrible!

She picked out a ten-carat yellow diamond ring, a Franck Muller watch, and diamond studs. The total priced out to be somewhere close to $300,000.

I'm sure you are wondering how a salesperson handles big sales. I was fairly new there, but I had my share of very large sales before I entered the Golden Bars. You learned to never act flustered. Besides, after all the wise cracks from the peanut gallery in the back room, it's going nowhere, right.?

Joseph gave me a price of $20,000 off the total. Vasha comes flying down the stairs to survey who she is. She had an ass you could play piano on from sitting and snacking all day (my mother's famous line if you were heavy in the rear department.) She wore a variety of blonde wigs, low cut blouses and tight sweaters. Her nose was on the large side, and you wish you could put quarters in it (like a piggy bank), that way you could have a good amount of money saved.

She looked at me and said her famous line, "Sweetie, darling does she know this is expensive jewelry?"

I wanted to say listen bitch do you think I just started in this business? Of course I didn't say that. I simply said, "She has a boyfriend."

Everyone in the back room repeated the famous line, "SHE HAS A BOYFRIEND!" They were all looking at the monitor in the office. They all were saying very nasty things and making snide jokes.

I was getting angry. I didn't know this woman, but can you not at least show some respect for a potential client? Joseph looked at me and saw how angry I was and how I was trying to contain myself. He told me I had just started.

"This is the way it is. People are jealous and love to make fun of the clients, especially attractive women, because there is always a story. You will learn. It will be worse when the old man comes back. You had better develop a tough skin because this crap goes on all the time."

I shook my head. I thought to myself he is the only kind person and guess what, I was correct. I went out of the main showroom and into the office where I had taken her when she first started looking at very expensive items.

I told her the price and she said, "Please write it down on your card. I will ask my boyfriend." I did as she asked. We give out a lot of cards. Some become sales and some do not.

After she left, they were still talking about her in the back room.

"I bet she has sore knees." said the Bahamian secretary, Galy. The back office erupts in laughter, and everyone is having a great time.

David Stubl said, "I bet she has good vowel control." Which I guessed was another nasty comment.

Vasha said to me, "This happens all the time honey Gia."

I was aghast that people could say such things! Welcome to C&F jewelers. If you have no money, we don't care. If you are a nice person, we don't care. If you don't have a check or credit card, then we care! (This was a line from Johnny Carson that Joseph changed around) It sums up the way everyone acted at the clients expense.

After that exchange, I was ready to go home. To make matters worse the boss called from Europe. There was more laughter and dirty jokes.

Vasha said to me, "If you sell anything we will buy you a bottle of champagne."

"Thanks." I said and walked out of the back room.

I went to sit down at my desk and the older woman that made the crack about the cheap chicken came over to me and apologized. She told me, "I just wanted to help you but after a while everyone got very nasty. You are new. I'm sorry, you did not deserve that. Let me tell you Gia when the old man comes back it gets much worse! There is no right here, only wrong."

I didn't quite understand that, but I learned quickly. She and I became good friends, and she helped me learn about C&F. She was close to 70 and had been there for twenty plus years. Another lady I got along with was also older and had been there for over forty years. Her name was Gail, but they called her G.G., which were her initials. She had a lot of clients but remember it didn't matter, because Bernard did not pay commissions. He never paid her much and it used to infuriate Joseph Brickmann. He was all about treating everyone the same and respectfully. Bernard Stein played favorites with HIS people.

If you were one of the chosen few, you could get away with almost anything. If a sales associate was a favorite, you could make mistakes or be allowed extra days off. I learned later you could also be a thief! We will get into that soon. Gail was busy, knowledgeable and kind to almost everyone. You could not help but like her. She always wore a shawl because he kept the showroom like Antarctica. She was tall and thin and had osteoporosis. Her back was rather slightly sloped. As I said, we called her by her initials GG.

I remember a day when a known client's daughter visited to purchase a watch. She was pushing a buggy and showing off her new baby. GG waited on her as she always waited on her and her entire family. She would never hurt anyone's feelings. She loved babies and always loved to coo and admire them. One thing about GG she never lied. After being around her for a while I realized how much she truly loved babies. She always had comments like, 'Oh, your baby is so beautiful.' or 'Oh what beautiful blue eyes!'

This day she took a look into the buggy and instead of the usual compliments she was known for, she simply said, "Now that's a baby!"

I asked her about her comment, when the client left the salon and she cackled to me. "Oh you caught that?

Listen Gia I never lie. You know I love children. This poor baby was the ugliest infant I've ever seen. Should I lie and say oh what a beautiful angel? If you say simply, 'Now that's a baby!' you are not telling a lie." I never forgot that wonderful statement.

The other person on the floor was an elderly lady that was my friend, and I had known her from my first job. She was an impeccable dresser and wise cracking funny lady.

She said to me after I thanked her for helping me get the job. "You will take back the thank you. This place is no walk in the park as you will soon find out!"

Of course I had no idea what I was in for, but I learned quickly. Her name was Yvette. It was amazing that she still remembered me! I found out that this industry is very small, and you know everyone!

Episode 16:

The Boss Returns

Mr. Stein came back from his buying trip with his wife and Julie. They bought a lot of gorgeous things, and we were allowed to wear all the goodies, because that is how we sold things.

Not to bounce around, but about three days after they returned, Mr. Stein took me into his office because apparently someone told him how I took my time with Barbi. He gave me this long talk about how I had wasted my time with a woman who had no idea of buying anything!

I looked at him and said "Never judge a book by its cover, Mr. Stein! Just because some people thought she was a loser she could be a potentially good client. You never know."

He started calling me by my last name. This was usually when he was annoyed with me. "Nichols you are new, and you could have spent your time better." I heard that a lot!

Ok, that being said I took the nasty comment, put it on the shelf, and thought to myself, I will never stop treating people like they do not matter! About a week later guess what? Barbi came back into the salon and asked for me.

Mr. Stein was watching the monitor and said "Nichols, you started something and now we will never get rid of this piece of dreck." (that is Yiddish meaning shit)

I rolled my eyes and said, "I will take care of it Mr. Stein. "

She looked at the pieces again and said to me, "I want to thank you for your kind treatment of me. I was a little intimidated by the looks of this place and you made me feel comfortable."

I said, "You never have to feel that way and I enjoy showing pretty things. You are always welcome here."

She smiled and thanked me again and said, "The man I am seeing is going to buy everything you have shown me. Can you please give me the special price again? I lost your card with the prices."

I smiled and walked into the back room where Julie, Mr. Stein and the whole back room were laughing and gossiping about the two of us. There were nasty comments about her being more on her knees than her feet. I heard the comment and opened up such a mouth about prejudging people and that their comments were sickening. I soon learned this was the way it was. Everyone had something unkind to say.

I waited for all the comments to end. "I heard from everyone back there. It looks like she is buying everything! Eight mouths hit the floor."

When they finally composed themselves, they said in unison, "How is she paying?"

I said, "I didn't ask but needed to get the price I gave her again so she could tell her boyfriend." I went to the book where we had to write all prices given and looked up the information.

Mr. Stein called Vasha downstairs and told her the story. "I remember this woman." she said in her thick fake Polish accent. "Is she for real?"

"Nichols seems to think so." he said.

She straightened her blonde wig and pulled her sweater down and said, "I will find out."

"Remember," I shot back, "you will owe me champagne."

Out Vasha went into the office where Barbi was seated and said, "Sweetie darling, how would you like to pay?"

"Oh I'm not sure," she said innocently, "so I guess I better call him. Can I use your phone please?"

"Certainly, help yourself. We are here to help you."

She gets up and goes into the back and I follow her closely, so as not to miss any exchange.

Vasha told Mr. Stein, "She doesn't know how he is going to pay." Laughter filled the back room, and my face got very red. I was angry that this is how they treat people and also because now they snicker like I'm stupid.

"Nichols gave her this itemized statement, so we are all clear on this business."

It was a 10ct fancy yellow diamond SI1 for $180,000. Diamond Stud earrings total carat weight 3 CT's G color SI1 $30,000, and a Franch Muller watch $45,000. A small diamond pendant was $15,000. Total price without taxes, $270,000. This was the special price given to her because the items were discounted.

Of course I would give her all the documents associated with the specific pieces but that comes after payment.

More laughter followed. I turned on my heels and Vasha followed me back to the office. I gave her the itemized statement. She gave her boyfriend all the details. He asked to speak to the person taking payment and the bookkeeper, Vasha, got back on the phone.

Conversation went as follows.

"Sir, this is an awfully large sum of money. We cannot take a credit card for the total amount."

They exchanged some words, and he said he would put a deposit down in order to hold the items. He would be doing a bank transfer of funds for the balance. Vasha got her big ass out of the chair, took the credit card number and walked into the back room.

I proceeded to thank Barbi for her business and told her I would be contacting her for the shipping address. She had a home outside the State of Illinois. She wanted to ship all the items to her other home.

She looked at me and said, "This transaction will go through in case you are worried."

"Never entered my mind." I said.

She should have known what was going on in the back room. When someone of good money or notoriety, or dubious reputation, Hollywood types visit, the back room is busy watching the monitors. They are all making bets on whatever you can imagine. They do not know how to make kind comments! Everything is a nasty slur. If this poor woman had heard them, she would have said go 'Fuck off! You all are jerks, and I will take my business down the street.'

She left and I was not happy thinking about what I was about to hear.

Vasha was the first to open her big mouth. "Sweetie, darling. Do you suppose we will see the rest of the money?"

Mr. Asswipe said, "I bet she really gives a good blow job!"

The queen bitch Julie said, "Why do you think she came in wearing jeans? Her knees are so red they look like Christmas. Ha, Ha, He, He!"

"Young lady it looks as if you might have a sale here, but I will reserve my congratulations until the check clears."

I didn't expect them to be nice, but this was a new low. In my history of working in the high-end jewelry business I've never heard people speak with such disrespect about a nice customer.

Approximately, three days later the troll Vasha called me into her office and announced I should tell the boss the money was transferred. I didn't want to hear the profanity again, but I knew after my first experience this would soon become common. Let's see how we can degrade a client. Let's go low!

He looked at me and said "Congratulations." and that was it!

I think secretly he was upset that she was a legitimate client. I learned NEVER JUDGE A BOOK BY ITS COVER. He wanted to have more fun with it all, because if there was one thing he didn't need it was money! On some very sick level Bernard Stein was in the business to be busy. The man didn't care if he sold something or not. This was definitely a new experience for me.

I happily called the client and told her the great news. She laughed and said, "I told you!"

She then invited me over for a glass of wine. I was flattered and said, "Thank you. I would love it!"

Of course I never said a word to the Super Rat Pack in the back.

Episode 17:

My Kind of Town

That evening, I went across the street to a very swanky address on Lake Shore Drive. I had to be announced, and the doormen were very familiar with my client. He told me to go right up.

She had the door ajar and yelled out. "Gia come on in."

Wow! Did I get an eyeful! The elegance was a knockout! It bordered slightly over the top but who cared, it was awesome. The most impressive part was the views. They were South, West and East. She was dressed up to go out. I told her I needed to have her come into the salon to be ring sized. Also, to get a mailing address to send the items she purchased.

She was so friendly and invited me out to dinner at a famous steak house on Rush Street. The Place was known as a hangout for important rich people. The mob and entertainers, when they are in town, made it their number one stop. Women loved it because it was a good possibility you would meet someone of importance and with money. Of course, a lot of flakes hung out there. Men would look for a partner for the evening. The women looked for husbands. They all had their reasons. It was a very posh setting with dark lighting and waiters that wore long aprons and were extremely discreet. Years ago, I went there for dinner with my ex-husband. It was quite the place.

"It's kind of pricey for me and I might see some clients. Also, I'm dressed for work."

Barbi laughed and said, "It's my treat for all your help. We can split a meal and have a glass of wine, and it would be quite affordable. Plus, you are not married. You never know you might meet someone."

"I'm dressed for work." I repeated in a downcast way.

"Take off your blazer and show some cleavage and you are all set."

I laughed and said, "Okay."

Before we left, she had to check her computer and told me she was on Match Your Life .com and wanted to check to see if anyone had written to her. I thought to myself. I thought she had a boyfriend. I decided to say nothing. I did not know her that well, to ask any questions.

She then took me on a tour of her apartment. Let's start with the living room. It had beige tones and gold accents. There were beautiful exotic Persian Rugs. An elegant couch that went from one end of the room to the middle of the room. In a shade of turquoise that matched her beautiful eyes. Throw pillows were scattered not only for comfort but they gave a very dressy elegant accent. Mirrors in gold were on the walls with beautiful pictures in between. The kitchen was open to the living room and that was gorgeous as well! There wasn't one detail that was not perfect. Next to the kitchen was a small tasteful bar, filled with imported crystal decanters. Down the hallway was the guest bedroom. The bedroom of course was tastefully done but less grand than the living room. The guest bathroom was marble and elegant in an understated way. There was a large picture of her and a young boy. I assumed it was a relative. The master bedroom, in all its glory, was next to the guest bedroom. Her bed was placed on a platform with faux mink. Or was it real? A beautiful Venetian chandelier was in the middle of the ceiling. It was over the top, but it suited her. The Master Bath was amazing in honey Onyx. Mirrors were everywhere. The master closet was a room itself. All her clothes were organized by type and color. It looked like she had a special decorator to organize her closet.

I didn't want to pry and ask questions about how she acquired all this wealth. I didn't have to. She told me her whole unbelievable story. She had met this man on a dating site. They developed a relationship of only conversation. Over several months of talking, he fell madly in love with her and wanted to buy her anything she wanted. I never met a more honest individual. She said she thought he was a hunter. He mentioned he had been in some kind of accident, and she was his fantasy. He had money from either the accident or he was rich. She didn't ask. The thing was, she had never met him. He was nervous about coming into the city. She thought he had some kind of disfigurement. They had a relationship only via the phone.

In fact she told me, he was the one that had bought her not only the apartment but the contents in the apartment. He also purchased all the jewelry I sold her! Well knock me out and call me crazy! I had never heard of a story like this but looking at her, I could believe it! I am 5 feet two inches. Streaked honey blonde hair with a tiny figure, big brown eyes. She was 5'7 inches with honey blonde hair and a size 6. Her eyes were turquoise and would stop anyone in their tracks. She resembled a movie star whose identity I cannot reveal. Together we looked pretty darn good. However, she was a show stopper!

She continued to tell me about Dirk, her boyfriend. He would make an excuse every time she would bring up getting together. He never suggested she should come to his place or meet in the suburbs. He loved her like an untouchable goddess. She thought if he wasn't disfigured, he had some kind of phobia. It was a story that was so far-fetched. If you didn't see her, you would call her a liar.

She asked me to have a seat while she changed. She changed into a short tasteful skirt with a leather blazer. Under the blazer she wore a seductive blouse. She put on very sexy boots that made her look like a tall, gorgeous model. I looked like I was going to work next to her. She threw back her flowing hair laughing and told me to take off the blazer and put on more makeup.

This began a friendship that spawned 20 plus years. Barbi was a down to earth beautiful woman. Men wood get whiplash turning their heads when she walks into a restaurant or bar.

That night she introduced me to so many people. She knew many men, women and couples. Everyone had a story, and she knew them all. The hostess at the restaurant was a model type just like Barbi, only a little taller. I felt like I was standing in a hole next to them both. She had natural jet-black hair with the greenest eyes. She was stunning!

I learned so many stories that night about the people that were there. They came for a great meal and to be noticed.

About 8pm I said, "It's getting late, and I must go home. I have to work in the morning."

Barbi asked me if I had a boyfriend. I told her I was seeing someone. He was a European. I saw him every month. We had traveled together to many places. I told her all about him. She asked me what do you do in between? I told her I went to work and sang in small cabarets. This was a full-time schedule. She told me I need to go on a dating site and meet other men. She asked me about my singing, and I told her it was my passion, and the jewelry business was how I lived and supported myself. How great it is that you sing, and asked me what kind of music? Mostly Jazz and Blues.

I had to make a choice. It was to sing and starve or sing when I can and hold a job. I also sang in many different languages. I sang in Greek of course, plus French, Italian and Spanish.

"Gia, my dear, you need to find a man that will take care of you and then you could sing and be a lady of leisure."

I told her that "If I find a man that I really love, I want to get married. I don't want to be supported by anyone."

She said "We are alike in many ways and yet we are very different in so many ways. In any case," she said, "the way to find a good man was on these dating sites!"

I'm not very tech savvy but she blew it off and said, "I will show you how to do it."

We hugged each other and I walked the three blocks home, while she crossed the street and walked home.

Episode 18:

C&F

The next day at work, the jokes continued. I went to speak to Joe Brickmann.

"Joe, how can people be so damn disrespectful."

He looked at me and said, "You have been here a couple of months, and you have just gotten a taste of how low they can go. There is a simple phrase we use up in the loft here right Rosa, Jax? There is no right here at C&F only wrong. Unless you are one of the chosen few."

"Funny," I said, "that is just what GG said down on the floor the other day."

"It's the Christians against the gladiators. Let me give you a hint." Joe said. "It's just like they threw the Christians to the wild animals. If you make a mistake, you will be thrown into the arena."

"Thanks." I turned and said as I walked downstairs.

I had been there almost a year and really was getting into the swing of things. Someone comes in and if they are a known client they get a good discount. Also, if Stein likes them or they are personal friends they also get a special price. If they come in just off the street and no one knows them they get a different discount. There is no rule. It depends on the OLD MAN. This is the way he runs his business. The only rule is his rule!

Many times, people come into the Salon to waste time and kick tires as we say. Make sure if they look at something and a price is given you write it down in the famous black book. If by some chance they come back and want to purchase that item or take another look, you had better have written all the information in the book, or you will wish you were dead!

He will belittle you and yell at you like an abused wife. He will go easy on you only if you are one of his chosen salespeople. As I was a Christian (Buddhist) I was in the group that goes into the arena. Also, for any item over $5,000.00 You had better take the client into a private room. When you do that the people in the back Stein, (The old man) Julie, David, Myron could watch what was going on.

I forgot to mention Myron would also do inventory. He had very little personality. He spent most of the day looking at his computer. He was capable of wise cracks as well.

After October, we start to gear up for the Christmas season. The merchandise that came in was unbelievable. Every kind of beautiful gemstone you could imagine! There were ropes of diamonds by the yard bracelets, earrings, anything imaginable. Bernard Stein liked the salespeople to wear the merchandise in the store so the clients could check it out on a person.

I was busy most days but, in the evening, at least three times a week, I would meet Barbi for dinner or drinks at a few of our favorite places. Our favorite was The Place. It definitely was the place to be seen and maybe see someone very special. By this time, I started to get to know her wealthy friends. Many of them came into the store to see me along with their boyfriends, husbands, and whatever. There were plenty of whatever's too!

My Israeli boyfriend, Michael, whom I met from a previous job, would come in as often as he could, and we went on many fun trips. We visited Los Angeles, New York and Paris. We went skiing in Gstaad. He spoke many languages, and we always had a great time together.

One day he sat looking at me and said, "Gia I need to speak with you about something."

"Ok," I said, "what is it?"

"We had carried out a relationship that lasted over two years. Listen, I'm crazy about you and I think you know that."

"I'm in love with you too." I answered.

"We have never had any intense discussion about our future together. We have had lots of fun on our trips together, but I knew I wanted more." he said.

We had fun for sure however, I couldn't see myself living in Israel. It was exciting seeing places I had visited with my crazy ex-husband. The difference was that here was a nice somewhat normal man. However, there was never anything really deep about our discussions. There was plenty of passion and he had an appetite for sex that matched my own. It was also exciting because we would spend time together. Our trips would last weekends and at the most ten days. He would tell me about his family in Israel. We talked about his work which involved the government. He couldn't tell me specific details. It was an unusual relationship. We had passion, fun but something was lacking. I loved him but I wasn't in love with him.

To be truthful, I think a lot got lost in our ethnicity. Even though my ex-husband was partly Jewish, this man was very religious. He kept kosher, which never bothered me. We ate in special restaurants. Our lives were definitely different. If I had to live in Israel, I don't think it would work. Before I started to think about anything, I thought let's see what's on his mind.

"Listen, Gia, the age difference between us doesn't bother me. As far as you being a Christian Orthodox (Buddhist) which I find amusing, I think living in Israel would not be a problem for us. You would adapt to my religion because you already know about the Jewish Orthodox faith."

Ok, I'm thinking this will not work. I don't like being told what we will do. That is a decision to be made by the two of us. Then he really drops the hammer.

"Gia, it's important for me to have a child. We don't need many but one we must have."

"Listen, Michael, I'm pushing forty-six and you are only thirty-six."

"Yes," he said, "but as we know everyone thinks you are my age or younger. You act younger than me and have much more energy."

"Thank you," Michael, "but I cannot have any more children at forty-six!"

"People do have children at forty-six so don't be absurd." he continued.

"Michael, I've told you I cannot have children because it is physically impossible. I had a hysterectomy when I was forty-one years of age." It was as if I threw ice water in his face.

"Gia, why have you not told me about this before? You know I'm in love. Why didn't you tell me?" His face was as red as a beet!

"Michael, you never asked me. We never had any talk about marriage before!"

"I have to go to my hotel and think about this!" he said. "I'm very upset!"

He got a taxi, took me home and left right away. Usually when he would visit me in Chicago, he would call me if he went back to his hotel to sleep, which hardly ever happened. He stayed overnight most times.

The next morning, he called me and said, "May I come over to see you please?"

Why so formal I thought. "Sure." I answered.

He took a few minutes to arrive and immediately took me in his arms. "Darling Gia, I have the answer. I was awake most of the night thinking about a solution for us."

I sat down. He began, "I love you more than you could possibly know. From the first moment I saw you,

I knew you were the person for me. You know I'm an Orthodox Jew. The biggest deal for an Orthodox Jewish family is to have a child. Since you cannot have children and I refuse to give you up, there is a solution. You will live like a queen in Florida. I will buy you a home there and you can retire there at 46. I will marry a Jewish girl and have one child. Until the child is older, I will commute between Israel and Florida. When I travel you will meet me, and we will go where I have to work. When I finish my work, we will go back. You will go to Florida, and I will go to Israel."

I looked at him and said, "It may work for you. However, it will not work for me. I do not share men. I will not be a mistress. If you are married, you will not see me. It is all or nothing."

He raised his voice telling me I was being unreasonable. I quietly walked over to the door, opened it and said, "Goodbye and good luck!"

He looked at me in disbelief. "I will not give you up."

"I already gave you up," I said. "Please leave."

He tried to contact me a couple of times after that, but I would not answer.

I related the whole story to Barbi, and she could not believe it! We had become pretty good friends, and I had to tell someone.

"Some women think that situation is ideal." she said.

"Not me." I replied.

That is the end of this story.

Episode 19:

Moving On

One night Barbi said, "Come over we are putting you right on MatchPeopleRight.com."

I decided to give it a try and went over to her house. I put on five current pictures and filled out an entire profile on myself. That was that!

"You want to marry, and I do not! We will find you exactly what it is you want!" I was dubious but decided to give it a try.

Work progressed, and in the evenings, I would scout out profiles of would-be perfect types. It was entertaining if nothing else.

Barbi gave me her rules. "After you feel comfortable enough, give him your phone number. After you talk with him five or six times and feel he's not full of shit, take the next step. Make plans to meet him in a public place. You will go there and have a drink. You will attempt to pay for your drink if you like him. If he lets you, scratch him off the list. I don't care how much you may like him. If he cannot buy you a drink, fuck him! Under no circumstances will you let him drive you home. If you like him, tell him to call you and make a date. There are no guarantees but always pick a known place and never drink too much. I do not want you to become a statistic."

I was nervous but she knew the ropes. I was naive so I trusted her.

Work was going well. It seemed the years were ticking by quickly. I was selling a good amount. It was of course, not without drama there. You had a lunatic for a boss constantly drilling you, with the same old questions. Who is it? Did he ask for me? What does he want to spend? He would turn to Galy or Julie, who ever happened to be near and if he knew them, he would tell them their story. More insults would follow.

One time he had me bring a designer object the client called about. He knew the client, but they were not special enough for him to get off his dead ass. He took the piece and marked it up twenty percent. He would then tell me to give them a fifteen percent discount off the tagged price. This was a common occurrence. If he knew them, he would say put them in an office. I'll have to take care of them. Then he would turn to Julie and say this must be the future Mrs. Number Three. The gossiping would start. There was more bullshit flying in that back room than ever happened on the floor or in any other office.

Sometimes it was funny but mostly it was revolting.

Episode 20:

Mishaps Here and There

If it was a really good day, Mr. Stein's son Tom would grace us with his presence. He was a weird, slightly off, kind of fellow. Supposedly, he knew how to really sell diamonds. If he was there and a cold caller would come in and Joe wasn't available, Mr. Stein would yell to call Tom down. We would prefer to show loose diamonds. The client could decide how he wanted to mount it.

I walked by the open office and there was Tom showing a two-carat diamond. The client suddenly walked out of the office and left. After about three or four minutes, Tom casually came out and said, "Where is the client?"

Our gay security guard Lucy, who I loved because she was always on target and had a great sense of humor was on duty. She answered back to Tom. "What is going on?"

He turned ashen and said, "The client simply got up, took the tweezers holding the diamond and said,

'I'll take this one.' With that statement he quietly walked out."

Lucy took off on foot like a bat out of hell! Running down Michigan Avenue after the crook!

Joe said to Tom, "Why did you wait so long?"

"I don't know. I thought he wanted to see it in natural sunlight." Tom was a little weird and slow. Mr. Stein was a little peeved but that was his son so nothing else was mentioned. I'm glad it wasn't me! Lucy never caught him. That was that.

On another day, Julie, his star salesperson, was showing diamonds. As usual she loved to run her mouth. Oh, I never mentioned her favorite pastime was drinking wine of any kind. If you started talking about wine, she forgot about everything else. Food was a close second. A number one rule was of course never leave the goods with a client even if you knew them. You would simply make an excuse to take the tray with you. Never make the client think you do not trust them. We were there to make the client feel like they were a friend. Supposedly, the people in the back room were watching what was going on. If the client left the office the guards were on the floor. They were always on the ball to watch everything on the main showroom floor.

That day, Julie started running her mouth and was not watching her inventory very well. We were only supposed to have a maximum of three loose diamonds on the tray. We always kept the diamond papers at hand to carefully re-wrap the diamond back in the individual paper where it belonged. Julie was a favorite and didn't have to follow the rules. Joe use to joke that a long time ago he suspected that when Julie was very young and started working at C&F she was very pretty. Not paunchy, like she was now, from drinking too much after hours.

She had an affair with Bernard Stein. It didn't last long. Mrs. Stein watched Bern like a hawk. If she thought he was unfaithful she would have, to put it bluntly, cut off his balls. She never left him alone on buying trips either.

Anyway, Bernard Stein made Julie his goddess. Any questions, he always asked her, not Joseph. He trusted her with his life.

"Julie," he would say when he got excited, "what should I do?" Of course he always foamed at the mouth and could spit across the room and hit twenty people easily.

Well, Bern you should do this or that she would say and 99% of the time he listened to her. Regarding the spitting, everyone knew not to stand too close to him. When he caught a cold, everyone caught it. We passed that cold around the office all the time!

That day she started talking about this or that. She was showing more than three diamonds and was talking about this restaurant or some other restaurant. She ran her mouth like a motor boat and was not paying attention. What else is new? Also, the customer was a well-known client. This made it worse. When she returned to the back room, she threw the tray at Joe to put it away for her because she already had another client come in.

Kiss, kiss. "Hi Lois, how are you?" She was on to the next one. You would think she was the hottest salesperson there. Next to Bernard Stein she was it. She had been with him for over 20 years. Whoever he knew, she knew. He knew everyone in Chicago. Including mayors, governors, society people, mobsters, entertainment people. They knew everyone! She comes back from the floor and starts telling Bernard Lois's story. This is how it always went. It was gossip, gossip and then more bullshit.

Joe told her he was missing a diamond, although the paper was there. One thing you always knew about Joseph Brickmann, he was as honest as the day was long. He had worked for Mr. Stein's father years ago. He was the most knowledgeable at the store and almost never made mistakes.

Julie looked at him aghast. "Oh shit, let's go into the office. Has anyone been in the number two office?" she piped out on the floor.

We all knew what that meant. It seemed something was amiss. Each one of us went flying back in the back office to find out what was up. Sure enough a paper and no diamond. We closed that office and called Romero downstairs. Romero had been with Mr. Stein for years. He did every errand you could think of. The people that worked for Mr. Stein had been there for more years than you could count. Mr. Stein was pushing eighty plus years and had been in the business for fifty plus years.

Poor Romero, he was always the first one they called for every shit bit of work. He and Julie sealed off the room and started going over it with a fine-tooth comb. Julie's face was red as a beet. It looked as if she had been on a bender for sure.

It took hours but they found it. She had been careless as usual. The diamond was in the corner of the room behind a chair leg. This was typical for her. Mr. Stein was miffed. Just like Tom's mishap, Julie could do no wrong. Even if she lost it, he would not be upset with her. He never lost his temper with her no matter what happened.

Julie had the best of the best of Mr. Stein's clients. A very large Urban developer and his wife were favorites of hers. He wasn't just large in girth but extremely wealthy. His wife was from Vienna. She was elegant and had arrogant airs about her. Julie acted as if they were best friends. She did this with many of Mr. Stein's clients. I always assumed, even though he was so much older than she was, that she met him in Europe. He bought her only the very best. She didn't like to mix with ordinary salespeople, but she was nice to me. One time, Julie wasn't immediately available to wait on her and she asked for me. When Julie heard I was assisting Madame Grendl she dropped what she was doing and went flying to her.

She threw me a dirty look and said very softly, "She sees only me, got that?"

"Sure," I said. "I was trying to be helpful."

That day, she ordered an amazing double rope of diamonds. When it finally came into the store and she picked it up, she loved it and proudly wore it that night to dinner to be seen by society's best.

I was having dinner with Barbi, of course at our favorite place.

When she walked by me, she stopped at our table and said hi to me. I almost fell over. She smiled at Barbi but made no comment. She then continued walking to her table where her husband and his group were waiting.

"Wow!" I said to Barbi. "Grendl so and so actually said hi to me."

"Okay," Barbi said. Continuing to look at the menu, she seemed unimpressed.

"That's one of Julie Coyle's best clients. You know who her husband is?"

Barbi put her menu down and looked amused. "So you think she is this very special lady, eh? "

"Yes," I replied.

"Actually, she used to be a receptionist in this office down the street near her future husband's office. He saw her and liked what he saw. Next thing I hear, he's looking for another girl to do a three way with her!"

"No way," I said.

"She's an aristocrat from Vienna."

"Really?"

"Why do you think she didn't acknowledge me? She knows me too well and let's leave it at that. I knew her when she was always nice. Now she is quite respectable and wouldn't remember me. I know her whole story. Her husband was a really freaky guy when he was younger. By the way, see her smile?"

"Yes," I said.

"Look closely. Her face has been pulled so tightly, that she can only smile half way." After that comment she continued looking at her menu. I got to learn a lot of people's stories. Her's was just one.

Episode 21:

More Mishaps

Let's go back to mishaps at C&F.

One time Mr. Stein was showing very large diamonds to one of his peeps, as we referred to them. He had more than three diamonds out, of course, and he left the room. Back and forth he went throwing diamonds and papers at Joe. If something went missing, who do you think they would blame? Not Mr. Stein of course. They would blame Joe. The client left as he wanted to think it over. However, he purchased a small trinket for the young lady. I really mean young.

This was a common occurrence. Many times, a rich old man would come in on a Friday night and purchase something for a sweet young thing with the promise that there would be more to come. Viagra should have been sold in the back room. Monday would come and half the time the article would be returned to stock. Mr. Stein was in a panic on Friday though. This was a lot of money.

He had so many diamonds out on the table. Back and forth he went. He was foaming at the mouth and spitting as usual at the prospect of a big sale looming. Poor Joe was trying to keep up but when Mr. Stein was on a roll, you couldn't keep up and believe me Joe was very fast. I believe it took us two hours, maybe longer, to find that one. Guess where this one was?

We accounted for every diamond except that one! When Sylvia Stein called him, he always took her calls but not this time. He told Jax to tell her he was busy. He never did that, so she knew something was up. Poor Jax couldn't even go to lunch or look at any porn that day. The only place that wasn't ransacked was Mr. Stein's office. We found a lot of things but not that big diamond.

Finally, Joe said, "You have a habit of putting things in your pockets. Empty the pockets in your coat and pants, anything you have touched."

Finally, he had him stand up. He looked at him and went down his pants leg. There it was in the cuff of his pants! A dazzling five carat round diamond. Mr. Stein thanked Joe, and everyone had a good laugh. We learned from that one. Always check his pant legs first. I will tell you some of the other places that we found stock another time.

Julie said she was going out for a few that night. Sylvia, Mr. Stein's wife, came running into the store because it could have been something she could have used! They were attending a special event, and she didn't want to miss out on anything.

She had one of everything, including a twelve-carat emerald cut diamond engagement ring, a fifteen-carat yellow diamond, and very large diamond earrings. She also had the most fabulous emerald cut emerald ring. You name it, she had it.

That night I had a dinner date with Barbi. I was very much on edge, but damn, I couldn't tell her what happened. We were always told if a story leaked out— he would know, and our job would be at stake. Believe me, he meant it.

That night Barbi and I went to The Place again. It became our go to hangout. They began to know me too. When I say hang out let me clarify. We would have a drink and then after about twenty minutes we would have dinner. We were always given booth one unless a movie star was in it.

Episode 22:

My Friend Barbi

You must understand, Barbi was a draw for every man over sixty. She was gorgeous but that was only half of it. She had personality and people knew her or wanted to know her. No she wasn't a whore. If she met someone, after dinner I would go home, and she would go out for drinks. She knew how to handle herself. There were very few times she had to call her doorman for help. She had a very quick wit.

She had many women acquaintances but one true friend and that was me. Many women were extremely jealous of her. She was not just beautiful, she was lucky. I would tell her not to trust this one because she was not a true friend. She learned from me too. Many times, she would tell me that I was right.

Now let's talk about the dating site we both used. It gets interesting. I had many dates. Not as many as her of course because there was only one Barbi. Different types of men were attracted to her. Barbi Brookman was a hot number! I was cute and slightly European sexy. She was a sizzler. You met her and you never forgot her!

Episode 23:

Oops, Mistakes Happen

The days flowed into each other. Sales were good. I was pretty lucky. I started having a great following. Mr. Stein took notice and one time he actually gave me a compliment. No more money was mentioned but he gave me a compliment. Joe said to me, money only comes if you threaten to quit or are one of his people.

Joe was always right. The man worked six days a week. He got Sundays off. Every time the poor man was due for a vacation, the old man would say not a good time. He would tell Joe to go in a few months. He would throw a little more money at him, and he kept working.

Honestly, we all depended on Joe Brickmann. Including Julie who made fun of him behind his back. When the question was about diamonds, fine jewelry or watches, he was the most knowledgeable. He had a dry sense of humor too. He would always say, "You are never right here. There is only wrong. Don't forget the gladiators always came out on top. The Christian's got their reward somewhere else."

The days passed and we were busy and then we were not busy. It was always the same. A late afternoon client with a friend came in one day. It was my up.

She came in and I saw that she and her friend were wearing loose-fitting blouses. I thought she was pregnant, but I never assumed anything. She stated that they were there to decide on a push present. That was a signal. She was pregnant. I did the old dog and pony show. She looked at just about everything. I was getting tired, and I guess it showed.

Finally, she said, "That's it! I will tell my husband!" I was so relieved. It was past closing, and I was finished. I turned to her friend and after it came out of my mouth, I wanted to fall through the floor.

"When are you going to start looking?" I said.

"I'm not pregnant." she stated.

They were both dressed the exact same way. I should have known better. You NEVER ask about her possibly being pregnant unless she tells you! Even if she delivers on the floor, YOU NEVER ASK.

I told her I was just trying to see how many of my feet would fit into my mouth. She was a great sport. After the usual groveling, I gave them some jewelry cleaner and some chocolates we had left over from a holiday. She laughed, I pretended to.

Episode 24:

Is There a Thief in the Building?

One morning I was doing our half fast inventory with one of the older women. I noticed something amiss. We had seven trays of large gold necklaces and now we have two. I told Mary, "Who tells the old man?"

She said to me, "I do after all I've been here longer than you. Before I do, let's talk about this." We sat down and went over every person and tried to think of a motive. We started at the top and covered each and every person. Finally, she said, "We should go to talk to Joe and see if he can figure it out."

We both felt as if we had cement on our feet. Joe was busy as usual. The look on our faces was enough for him to stop what he was doing. We explained the situation to him. Again, we went over every person starting with the front office.

Julie, she's not the kind of person who would steal. Also, she's very loyal. She's a drunk but not a thief. David

Stubl was Mr. Stein's right hand. He does the checking in of inventory and Myron sits next to him. Together they know what is coming in and going out. David has been working for Mr. Stein for over thirty years. He always stares at his computer. He never has much to say to anyone. Always loves the wisecracks. He and Julie have always been pretty tight. He has a wife and two kids, takes nice vacations. His kids go to private schools but he's one of the chosen few. He is paid quite well, so he's out.

Myron is not from the chosen people. Another one that doesn't say much but always joins in on the wise cracks. He had a wife and a daughter, and that's all I know. David had Been with Mr. Stein the longest. That was almost as long as Julie. Galy was the Bahamian lady who went after anyone with wise cracks as much as Julie. She had been with Mr. Stein a long time as well. She had money from her parents and lived very frugally.

Mary and I just couldn't figure it out. Joe went through the same people and then he went through the sales floor people. Vasha, the accountant was a pain in the ass, but she didn't touch the jewelry. Rosa checks the jewelry as it comes in from vendors, but she doesn't touch the old merchandise. Jax, he's more interested in being on his computer and if he's not shipping, he's looking at porn. The ones that looked guilty are the salespeople because they touch all the merchandise.

"Oh Joe, I need this job. I haven't touched anything!" I said.

He said to me, "Gia you're a Christian Buddhist. You are guilty already"! He laughed, but I cried, and he said, "Get a hold of yourself. Every salesperson here I know, and I would vouch for everyone."

"I have to tell Stein. Please be strong. I know all the people on the sales floor, and you are all good people. Be strong." he repeated.

Easy for him to say. I'm supporting a disabled veteran who is waiting to be classified 100 percent disabled. My son is a mess. I'm not a thief.

Again, Joe said, "Gia, calm yourself and don't say anything to anyone."

The next day he told Stein. The atomic bomb went off easier than this one. He started looking at all the salespeople as if we were guilty. I chanted all the time for an answer.

Julie said this in front of me. She told Bern in her twang, "I think you should look and question the newest salespeople first."

David Stubl replied, "It is something to think about."

I saw Joe Brickmann as we were closing and asked if I could have a few minutes of his time. He said sure, but before I started to tell him what was said, he said, "Gia listen, the back office is a loft and sound carries. I heard what that cow said to you. She is a jealous person. You are about two years younger than she is and you look 20 years younger. Just wait. I have my own ideas."

I went home that night and chanted and then cried myself to sleep. My son heard me and came into my bedroom. He was sleeping on my couch in the living room. I told him the whole story and swore him to secrecy.

"Don't worry mom," he said, "the truth always comes out."

The next day Mr. Stein had Yvette in his office with the door closed. She came out visibly upset and shook her head at me. After her, Mary went in. After Mary, then GG. She was near Mr. Stein's age and looked very old and withered. Slumped over because of osteoporosis she looked at me and gave out a cackle.

I looked worried. I asked myself why I was worried. I had taken nothing. I was still worried, but I wasn't going to show them. Jax the shipper looked at me as I went up to the lunch room. He always called me by my full name. Mr. Stein always did as well. "Gia Nichols stop worrying. We know you took nothing."

About three days later Joe Brickmann went into Mr. Stein's office and closed the door. Nothing was said for about a week. All of a sudden Joe comes into the store very early one morning. Then he went into Mr. Stein's office. We heard nothing for about a week, except snide remarks from Julie and David Stubl.

After another week, I went into the store and started setting up in the morning as usual. I heard raised voices and drawers being opened and banged shut. Then Joe Brickmann leaves his place at the top of the loft and puts his finger against his lips and tells me to stay on the sales floor. Don't come into the back room. About an hour later I see David Stubl with a briefcase leaving the building.

Mr. Stein makes an announcement. "We are going to forget what happened. Nothing more will be said to anyone."

Yvette went and sat down at her front table. There she quietly had a mini stroke. Mary went flying into Mr. Stein's office and told him what happened. He did not want her to leave her post. Joe comes flying down the stairs and checks poor Yvette. He called an ambulance, and she was carried out of the front door in a stretcher.

Mr. Stein was complaining that he had no more salespeople and Joe told him, "Stop right there. She is sick and of no use to you in her present condition. She is going to the hospital to be checked out." Joe, with his dry sense of humor said, "This is the way salespeople go out the door. They go on a stretcher, or in a body bag." It was not funny but everyone except me laughed.

As we were preparing to leave, Joe said he will talk with me later. Yvette is gone and David Stubl is gone, and it is quiet all day. The next day Julie is quiet for a change. No wisecracking from her, Mr. Stein or Galy. She was close to David and was shocked it was him.

Strange People are Regulars and the Story about the Thief

I got a client at about 3:00 pm and I had to take him into the office. Rather, It was a man alone shopping for his friend or wife. He was looking for a diamond bracelet, like a cuff. I couldn't find anything like he described so I tried to be creative. I asked him some questions about the very special person he had in mind for this gift.

I came out with a dog collar. It was thin and full of diamonds. Also, it was wide and rather mesh-like, delicate and pretty. He said to me, "I like it. She wanted a bracelet."

I said, "Well you could take it home and see what she thinks."

"No," he said. "I will call her, and she can come over and see what she thinks of it."

I went into the back office and was given the third degree by Mr. Stein. "Why did you show him that if he clearly told you he wanted a bracelet?"

"We didn't have what he wanted so I was trying to be creative and sell what we had. You always tell me this. I asked him about her likes and dislikes…"

He interrupted me. "So you show him a diamond dog collar?"

"It's not a dog collar, it is a mesh collar with diamonds." I stated. Just then I started getting concerned that my client was waiting for my return in the 2nd office.

Mr. Stein sighs and said, "Next time you get into a bind, call Julie or Mary." I shook my head and tried to maintain my dignity.

I walk back to the office. My client is kissing his girlfriend. They could have cared less that I was there. She was tall, dressed in black with her black hair piled high on her head. She had dark red full lips and was very sexy looking. He told her that we didn't have a bracelet like she wanted but that I found something that she might like.

She glanced down at the necklace and pursed her lips. "I will try it on, but it is not what I wanted." She had a slender neck so I thought I might get lucky. She put it on and stood up. Placing her legs astride she looked at him with a very sexy expression. She placed her hands on her hips and said, "Leo, perfect for S&M! What do you think? My black whip?" She then acts like I'm not there and strides him like a horse.

I got up and quietly left the office. My face was as red as a beet. Five minutes later I returned. "We will take it. Wrap it up. We are in a hurry." I took it from her and hurried to wrap it.

"My, my,." said Myron as we passed each other. "I saw what was going on. What was said, we couldn't hear?"

"None of your business." I shot back.

Mr. Stein said, "Gia Nichols nice sale. You didn't even give them a special price!"

"They were in a hurry. By the way, she didn't think of it as a dog collar." I smiled and left the room.

That evening Joe met me as I was leaving the salon. "Do you want to know what happened with the missing trays of gold necklaces?"

"Of course!" I said. "No one had said another word about it for two days."

"Let's meet my wife and go and have a cup of coffee." Joe never drank alcohol or coffee. He called Penny, his wife and we met at the corner coffee house.

"I'm sure you will hear some version of this in the next few days. I wanted to tell you the whole truth. The people in the back office all know. Rosa and Jax know because they sit next to me. This is the story. You know how frugal I am, right?"

Penny chimes that he is cheap. I should tell you Penny is a lovely lady who used to work for Mr. Stein but after five years she had enough. She now works for an antique dealer. She is about 5'5 inches tall. She has beautiful green eyes and is very pretty.

Penny continued on. "Joe always has ways of saving Mr. Stein money. He of course never says thank you but that's the nature of the beast. He is always taking Joe for granted. Many days at the bench he gets jobs that have-to-have pieces cut out of them. Such as a necklace or a bracelet. Many times, there are tiny pieces of gold left over. If the client doesn't ask for the scraps back, he throws them into a little box under his desk. When the box gets full, he transfers the gold into another box and then puts that into the safe upstairs. He then starts all over again filling the box up and transferring it into the other safe. When the box in the safe is full he calls one of our scrap metal people."

Joe then takes over. "Gia doesn't know about the scrap people. I will continue if you don't mind. There are many people we do business with that take our old gold. They weigh it and give us the money for it. I take the money and give it to Mr. Stein. I've been doing this for years, he said."

Penny then interjects. "Never a thank you, either."

"About four months ago, the scraps in the safe disappeared. I looked high and low for the box. I told Mr. Stein. He told me that it was not much money and to forget it. My feeling is money is money. I said nothing to anyone else. Jax and Rosa knew because I questioned them. They knew about it but forgot and both answered at the same time. 'Where is it? We haven't seen it.' At first, I thought I was losing my mind. I thought someone else knew about the old gold.

"After Mr. Stein went on his tirade about the missing necklaces. I started thinking about it all. He blamed all the new people first. You, in general. The people in the back office of course went along with him. I knew it was not that simple. Why would my old gold disappear as well? You didn't know anything about that. Only a few people knew. I went to him and said, 'This might be a stretch but if someone is fencing gold where would you go? You wouldn't go to a jeweler.' After a while suspicions would kick in. A scrap metal guy doesn't care about this if it's broken up!

"Just for the hell of it, do I have your permission to call our scrap metal people and check to see if anyone has brought in any gold? 'I think you are going out on a limb,' Mr. Stein said, 'but go ahead. Before I start giving lie detector tests, I will try anything.'

"Lie detector tests!" I said rather loudly.

"Hold on. Don't get upset and let me continue. I called three of the people we do business with and asked if anyone associated with us has been bringing in any scrap metal to sell. About a day later I got a call from Jenkins and Boyd. We send them a good amount of old gold," he explained.

"Mr. Boyd called and said for about the last year and eight months David Stubl had been bringing in large amounts of broken gold necklaces. They were broken in pieces. He also brought along my old gold from the upstairs safe." He continued on. "The necklaces were a mess. Still, I asked him, "Why didn't you call the store and ask me?' He said, 'David is a top manager and if he said the gold necklaces were not usable anymore, who am I to question it?'

"Mr. Stein talked to Mr. Boyd and the next day David was in Mr. Stein's office and spilled his guts like the rat he is. I always knew there was something very fishy about him. He always came in early with his briefcase. His angle was he took three or four of the necklaces at a time. He took out his trusty little hammer and then he broke up fine pieces of heavy gold necklaces. He didn't take too much at a time. However, after a while Mary noticed seven trays of gold turned into less than two. I noticed as well because she called me into the safe to count with her. How do you think he was able to afford fancy special schools for his kids and lavish vacations?

"Mr. Stein started to turn as red as a beet. David was one of the chosen few that sat in his inner circle. He would rather blame an innocent person than one of his own! By the time the salespeople came in, he had finished breaking up the gold. Then he put it into his briefcase."

My mouth hit the floor. "Oh my god! I could have gone to jail for that low life. Now what?"

"They both knew the same people at Steins country club. So he told Stubl, he will not prosecute him. However, you are no longer an employee of this store."

"Did he ask for him to pay him back?"

"No!"

"Did he call the police?"

"No!"

"Why?"

"He didn't want any publicity and let's not forget how wealthy Mr. Stein is. If it were you or me Gia, we would be sitting in jail. This is the sad reality. Now, let's see how he tells the staff about this one. Jax, Rosa and Mary all know about it already. Julie knows of course and so does everyone else in the back office."

"Poor Yvette had a stroke because he blamed her for bringing you into the store for a job." I started to tear up.

"Gia, stop, you are innocent. Yvette will be fine. David is gone. Let's just wait to hear how the boss handles telling everyone else. Remember, you know nothing."

The next day Mr. Stein called an employee meeting before the store opened for the day. He never mentioned who he suspected. He glossed over most of it. He had to tell us David was the culprit. He did not elaborate on any of the particulars. He said he fired him and of course he wanted no one to speak about this to anyone in the jewelry business. He would know where it came from. The end of the story was simply, get back to work.

Yvette came back to work in a week, and she was livid! Of course she said nothing to Stein. Like all of us she needed the job.

I said to myself, 'Thank you, Joe Brickmann. You are my angel.'

I got a call from Barbi just as I was leaving the store. "Are you busy?" she asked.

"No, it's been quite a day." I said.

"I have the cure." she shot back. "Come over when you are breaking out of prison, and we will go to The Place for dinner."

"I don't really feel like going out." I told her.

"All the more reason we are going." she said.

I headed out of Hell and walked across the street to her condo where a glass of wine was waiting for me. I couldn't tell her what happened, I just said there was a lot going on over there today.

She said, "You look like you have been through hell!"

"I have," I said, "but would rather not discuss it."

"Okay." she answered. "How are the dating sites going, she asked?"

"Who has time?" I answered back.

"Make time. Do you want to be there all your life?"

"No," I replied. "The computer dating sites are all full of shit," I said.

"Not all. Have a little faith."

"I will." I said.

"I will ask you questions next week. So get to it!"

Episode 26:

You feel Awful…
Let's Have Dinner

We went to dinner, and lo and behold there sat my boss with a top client who happened to be his dear friend. The man was one of the nicest people you could hope to meet. I do not know how he could be friends with the Steins. He was a very wealthy man like most of our clients but never looked down at salespeople, like a lot of clients did.

His wife, the second Mrs., had been married five times before. She hit the jackpot with him. He was kind, sweet, and rich. She led him around by the nose, but I guess he was happy. They were married longer than any of the other husbands she had. They were Mr. and Mrs. David Houseman, but they called him Skip. I had no idea why. Barbi waved to everyone at the table. I could just hear the questions tomorrow.

We shared a salmon dinner and had wine and salad. Of course, everyone as usual knew Barbi. The hostess and Barbi were good friends. Tall and curvy with green eyes. She had black hair cut short. Her name was Antoinette, but Barbi called her Toni.

As difficult as it is to believe she actually knew more people than Barbi. The mayor was a regular. He liked to sit in a back booth where no one could see him. The governor was also a regular when he was in town. Everyone and anyone knew the Place. The food was great, expensive and a place to be seen. Entertainers, when in town, always went there. Along with mobsters, gold diggers and the rich and famous. Toni on several occasions had to throw out the very obvious working girls who of course were regulars. Anyone that wanted to be noticed visited. Including Gia Nichols and Barbi Brookman.

A couple men Barbi knew stopped by our table and sat down and talked for about 30 minutes. One complained about his wife and how she always spent too much money.

"By the way, she was the one with the money." Barbi told me afterwards. They were both her friends.

He always acted like a big shot. I was annoyed. I had to put up with bull shit at the store.

"Why did we have to put up with this shit?"

"Well, they picked up our dinner check. You never know Gia my dear. This year's jerk could be next year's rich man.

"I would rather eat a piece of toast and have water

than put up with this bull shit." I said. "This goes on at work. Going out to dinner should be fun.

"Gia, sometimes you have to put up with a little bullshit. Listen and learn.

It was great to go home.

Episode 27:

MatchPeopleRight.Com

Barbi was always on my case about staying on Match-PeopleRight.com. I said, "What's the use? Most men are full of shit."

"No Gia, you have to weed out the assholes and be very careful what you think are the good ones. Remember, always in a public place."

I did go out after interviewing quite a few men. Some were nice and some were, of course, outright jerks. One experience taught me what Barbi warned me about.

We met in a public place as usual. He was charming and very surprised I actually looked like my pictures on the dating site. He tried to impress me as most men I had met. After our date, he offered to take me in a taxi to my apartment. I said no at first, per Barbi Brookman's instructions. After thinking about it, I thought a taxi was safe enough. I lived about seven blocks from the bar, but it was a cold evening, and I thought it should be okay.

As soon as the door was shut, he grabbed me and stuck his tongue in my mouth. I tried to push him away, but he was too strong. He held my head with his hands, and I struggled to free myself. It was the longest taxi ride I ever had! We got to the door. I grabbed the door lever and pushed myself out. I almost fell onto the street. He had the longest tongue, and it almost came with me! I ran to my apartment after asking the doorman not to allow anyone in after me. Two days later, the same guy called, and I did not take his call. He left a message.

"Hey, Gia, this is your wonderful date of two nights ago. How about dinner with me? We could go anywhere you want."

I never picked up the phone and eventually he got my message.

The next day, I told Barbi what had happened. She really got angry with me. Listen, unless you want to become a statistic you had better listen to what I tell you. She then told me to go buy two books called *Something Dating*, and the second book was *The Rules of Life*.

"Read them cover to cover. Do what they say, do what I tell you and you will be fine."

It never happened again because I became very cautious and extremely selective. I was never bored anymore. Anyway, I had my work at Cooper and Flux. I went out at least three times a week for a small dinner with Barbi. I got so busy. I forgot about my singing in cabarets. Music has always been my passion. I could not afford to make it my full-time work because singing gigs were sporadic. You cannot burn the proverbial candle at both ends and not burn out. On occasion, I would go to nursing homes and sing for charity.

My co-workers said, "Why do you do it?"

I said, "Because the people in the nursing homes are lonely. They appreciate people coming to entertain them. They are mostly in wheelchairs and can't walk out." I joked. "The truth is I got more from it than I gave. Most of the people knew all the songs I was singing because they were music from the 30's, 40's etc. they were so appreciative. I loved doing it. It made me so happy."

My week went on as usual. I thought about the internet dating site as a hobby. I met some nice people and some strange people. I was never bored with it. It was entertainment. Barbi and I continued our friendship. We enjoyed evenings out for dinner and lively conversation about some of her escapades.

Episode 28:

Mistakes Can Happen to Anyone

Barbi was never short on dates! Her stories could write another book. She once met a man that looked like a former President. She called him Bill (though not his name) and he wasn't the former President. They went out on a couple of dates. He started getting too pushy. She told him to hit the road. The last evening they were out together, she told him that she felt they were not well suited. He said, well, let's have dinner anyway.

On that night she said goodbye. She turned and did not realize he was following her. The doorman in her building was getting a taxi for another resident. He did not catch him sliding by the station. Next came the knock on her condo door. Not expecting to see him, she opened the door thinking it would be the doorman with packages.

Bill waltzes in and announces he would be making love to her. She calmly picked up the phone to call the doorman. The doorman was not at his station. Pretending to talk to him, she said to no one, please come up immediately. Meanwhile Bill had disrobed completely.

She turned around and there he stood in all his glory. She then tried to reason with him calmly. When that didn't work, she raised her voice. The chase began and she was the mouse! From room to room the chase continued. She could run pretty fast because he was pretty drunk!

Suddenly, he caught her, and the struggle began. My friend landed a right hook just as the doorman knocked on the door. Bill was down for the count. Then a fully dressed, somewhat out of breath Barbi answered the door. The doorman saw her number on his panel and went directly to her condo. He saw Bill on the floor out cold. He was stark naked but with an erection that looked like a flag! The doorman started laughing hysterically.

"Well Ms. Brookman, I guess you can take care of yourself!"

She said, "Please remove this drunk, crazy man."

By the time the doorman found Bill's clothes, he was regaining consciousness. Not seeing the doorman, he rubbed his chin. He looked up at Barbi and said, "Let's pick up where we left off."

James, the doorman, said to old Bill, "I want you to dress quickly. If you are not out of our sight in five minutes the police will be visiting you."

Faster than a speeding bullet, Bill was gone. James received a twenty-dollar tip. I laughed for about thirty minutes.

I said, "Maybe I should give you my book, Dating 101."

"We are not amused." she said.

In any case it all ended well. The story did not end there. For now, that was the last of Bill.

Episode 29:

More Employees!

Mr. Stein had been interviewing people for the sales floor. There were eight full-time salespeople. When we needed extra people, the back room would produce Julie and Joseph. For some reason, Mr. Stein now felt he didn't have enough coverage. The interview began.

Mr. Stein interviewed about ten people and decided to hire three. One was a young man who had worked in Manhattan for a watch company. The second candidate was an Asian man who had great experience in sales. The third person was a gorgeous blonde who had sales experience in jewelry. Mary complained to us all. "Why should Mr. Stein hire more sales staff when half the time, we are sitting around?"

"Maybe it's his ego?" I said.

"Bingo. Give that lady a gold star." said Joe, who had overheard us talking. "This whole business is about his ego. Listen," Joe continued, "when his old man passed away, Mr. Stein had enough money to never work again. He owned half of Wrigleyville. His own jewelry business had more money than any of these other jewelry stores. The old man died, and they immediately went into his store and threw out all the employees. Mr. Stein padlocked the doors and that was it."

"Joe, you worked for his father." I said. "What do you think he had in jewelry cash wise?"

"He had over 50 million, easily. The property, you can't put a price on it. This entire business right here is all about Bernard Stein's EGO. Yes, he makes money, sure. He enjoys working. This is the whole story. If it wasn't for his wife, he would never take a vacation. She had put her foot down, and he had no choice. Sylvia is his everything. She is his keeper, wife and warden of his crazy kids. You name it. Mr. Stein would work seven days a week if she would let him. This place is his soul. Julie is his everything as well."

"This is a strange environment." I answered Joe.

"You are just figuring it out Gia? We also have a motley crew here, Gia. Look at all of us. Julie is a drunk with little knowledge and a lot of bullshit. He listens to her about 100% of the time. As I told you, I think he had an affair or something with her years ago. He has this sick fixation with her. Everyone here has some issue, including me." he said.

"What's your issue Joe?"

"I like surviving and I'm cheap. I save as much as my wife lets me. Stein pays me well. Yes, I can do better. I'm comfortable here. When I finally have enough of all the bull shit around here, I will walk. Well, I guess we should all get back to work." GG and Mary chuckled. "We all have stories to tell, Gia. When you have been here a little longer you will learn everyone's particular reason for staying in an abusive atmosphere like this one."

Most people in the back office have been with Stein for over twenty years. They probably could not work anywhere else. Listen and learn. The two old ladies walked away. Laughing, they said, we should get ready for the new recruits.

The first person I met was Judy. She was a very attractive blonde, who had worked in jewelry stores. I think he hired her because he wanted some younger people. He mentioned Mary and GG were on their way to retirement. Judy had a great figure and knew it. She had a very pretty face and was considered sexy. Julie, of course, was nasty to her. Jealousy should have been her second name. She was sarcastic to most of the younger girls. Always challenging our abilities. Usually, she was a pig. She was the pig of choice, so we all learned, never cross her.

The next person was an Asian man named Yori. He was about forty years old and had experience in the business. He could also speak several languages. Lastly, was Daniel Saltzman. He had experience in watches and had worked in Manhattan. He was in his late twenty's but knew it all, or so he thought. Joe Brickmann could take him apart in two seconds. He was always watching him. Joe was a gemologist, horologist and had worked long and hard in the business. He had knowledge every-one wished they had. We all differed to Joe including the old man and Julie. They hated him. He didn't kiss their asses. They knew he was the smartest one there and went to him for everything. Behind his back, they made fun of him.

At Cooper and Flux everyone in the back office was somewhat nice but behind your back they ripped you apart. Sometimes, they would do it to your face. If you forgot to make a note of a client, or made an error of any kind, you were picked apart. Sometimes it was to your face. Stein's yelling was something to behold. You could never hear him yelling on the sales floor because the doors were solid. I think he planned it that way. He could beat you down and embarrass you. He and Julie made shit out of everyone. When he made a mistake and he made many, they were real doozies. However, no one dared to ever mention them. Julie was the same. The only one who could criticize her was Stein. He never did, though. When he caught her in a mistake, he would never reprimand her. She could never be wrong. One time she sent a very expensive string of Tahitian Pearls to a vendor, instead of the customer. We couldn't find out what happened to them. They were being restrung and should have gone back to the client. Instead, she sent them to a vendor that we dealt with for diamonds. She tried to blame Rosa or Jax for screwing up. Lucky for everyone the vendor called and questioned why we would send him pearls when he was waiting for a strand of diamonds? Did she apologize to Jax or Rosa for picking them apart? Hell no. She laughed and said to me, "Wasn't it lucky someone was honest."

Work went on as usual. Sales were going well. The new salespeople were settling into the routine. After the initial honeymoon stage where the old man talks to you like you matter, you graduate to the imbecile stage. Unless you are one of the chosen few, every mistake is magnified.

We all rejoiced when he would go with Julie and Mrs. Stein on a buying trip to either Switzerland or Italy. Joe would become the man in charge, and everything would run nice and smoothly. He would do this about two to three times a year.

GG had a great sale of a hundred thousand dollars to one of her clients, and Mary sold a watch for $35,000. It didn't matter how much you sold because no one was on commission. At the end of the year he would give you a bonus. Again, it didn't matter how much you sold. If you were a favorite, money flowed. If you were one of his gladiators, you were smiling from his generosity. I had asked for a raise and was told it was not a good year. Interesting, it was not a good year but we hired more people.

Episode 30:

The 60s Were Good, If You Remember Them

One very warm summer day, I was on the sales floor and a middle-aged man walked into the store with his friend. They had both been drinking and smelled of sweat. They walked over to the most expensive watch case. The man asked to see a Franch Muller watch. It had a price tag of about seventy-five thousand dollars. He asked me about the complications, and I gave him my sales pitch. I was explaining everything. One of the new men, Daniel interrupted me. He corrected a point I had made. Instead of the man focusing on the intruder who seemed to know more than I did. He asked me another question and I continued on. I thought that was extremely kind and unusual. I figured him out as a tire kicker and thought he was taking up my time. However, I treated every person like they were the president of a company. Also, I had nothing better to do. After a few more questions directed at me, Daniel or as I called him to the others, Mr. Peepers because he wore horn-rimmed glasses. and smoked like a chimney. Appearing like he spent a month on a starvation diet, you would think a wind could blow him over. He sounded miffed. He couldn't butt in, so he left.

The older man was still interested and asked his friend what he thought? His friend shrugged his shoulders and gave no opinion. I was ready to return the watch to the case and the man said he would take it. I glanced at his attire. Pre-judging I thought maybe he's trying to pull something. He then pulled out a Black American Express card and handed it to me. From my experiences of working at C&F and my other three jobs, if we didn't know the client, we could be a little skeptical if they made a large purchase.

I composed myself and walked quietly to the back. As the door slammed shut, I said to Myron, "I think this might be stolen."

He went through the usual drill. "Who is it?"

"If I knew him then I wouldn't guess it could be stolen, would I?"

"Did you give him a price?"

"No, he didn't ask for one." I said.

"Well, run it and see if it works."

I thought, you don't even give a shit. You all only care if it is a sale to report to Mr. Stein when he calls in for a report of what's going on. I ran it. It went through. Myron said, good sale.

I went back to the floor. The man called me by my name as I had given him my card thinking he would say, I will think about it.

He then said "Gia, if I send it to my office in Beverly Hills, I won't pay tax, right?"

My face became as red as a beet, and I was ashamed of myself. "Yes sir." I stammered hoping he couldn't read my mind.

I now returned to the back room and started to rewrite my sale, only without tax. I glanced at the name and a ton of bricks should have hit me square in the face. Wow! I couldn't believe I hadn't recognized him. He was the bass player and really the co-founder behind a 60's popular musical group. I would have recognized him if he had come in the way he was back then. Alas, the years and drugs, among other things, left a mark. He was a total gentleman!

When I called him Mr., he corrected me and said, "Please just call me Justin. You are a sweetheart. I will visit you again."

I wanted to ask him about the lead female singer. Had I mentioned her name, you would recognize the group immediately. Since he was so friendly I thought to myself, keep your mouth shut. He was a regular guy and a gentleman. Do not blow it by being star struck. If you want a story about star struck. I have a lot to tell you. Some I can talk about. Unfortunately, for most celebrities I cannot. People would not like to be mentioned by their name.

This is a story I can tell you. As I mentioned, I worked at the French company that was known first for its perfume and then its famous founder. They were also very well known for handbags and beautiful clothes. I worked there for a very short time. I met some interesting people. I'm going to go off my main story to tell you about one very special lady. The company had opened a very fine jewelry department. I was recruited to work there after I walked out on my second boss. It was before the time of sexual harassment not being tolerated. I left the French store because I had a high-profile client that ordered a special ring. It was $50,000. I was told by an employee in France that it would take six to eight weeks to receive. At the last minute, a famous figure skater who had won Gold at the Olympics wanted it and they pulled it from me to sell it to this famous skater. I decided the lost commission makes this job not desirable. I left in a huff and walked straight into Cooper and Flux. I was jumping from the frying pan into the fire, but I didn't know it at that time.

Okay, so back to my short French moment. Oui, Oui! I was having a down moment when I got word from the main salon that a famous celebrity was charging up a nice tidy sum in accessories. They wanted to know if one of us wanted to try and coax her into the fine jewelry salon. Everyone else was hesitant. Not yours truly. I loved trying to reach out to anyone, especially if they were a celebrity.

I started walking up the stairs that separated the fine jewelry from the main salon. I am not exaggerating this. I was met by a huge bodyguard. He tried blocking my way, but I pushed by him. He was wearing an earpiece, but that was not a deterrent! He weighed over 300 Lbs. Still I continued on. There she was!!!! Next to Tina Turner, my all-time idol, this lady was it for me! She had a floor length stone martin fur coat dragging on the floor and needed to hold on to the handrail to steady herself. I ignored the bodyguard as I reached the queen of soul!

"Miss Franklin! Miss Franklin!" I called out to this beautiful vision. She was not well. You could tell she was having a problem navigating. Her skin was lovely and for an older lady she was pretty with style! "Please, will you spend five minutes with me? My name is Gia Nichols. I would like to show you some very special things that would suit a lady of your stature. I work at our special fine jewelry department. I'm sure we could find something that you would love!!!!"

She looked at me. She gave me the biggest smile I have ever seen. "Baby, baby, you know I can't afford your price tags."

"Oh Miss Franklin, we have jewelry that starts at less than one of our special handbags."

"Honey, I would love nothing more. I'm on a tight budget right now."

She made me feel like I was ten feet tall. The bodyguard tried to remove me from her. She waved him back. She told me I was very sweet to come over and see her. Unfortunately, she couldn't possibly spend time right now.

I said, "I understand Miss Franklin. May I say you truly are the Queen of Soul, and I am a big fan." Instead of dismissing me with her hand. She thanked me, flashing that wonderful smile and said maybe next time baby.

I was floating back to the showroom, and though I had met a few rock stars, this lady had more class treating me like a special person than anyone else up to this point.

My boss said, "You were speaking to her for quite a while, any luck?"

I told her. "I just met the Queen of Soul, and you know, she is a queen! This was my wonderful luck."

Another time at the same store, I worked with a lady who was close to eighty years old. She worked in the shoe department. Her personality was humble, and she was as lovely as could be. At her age she moved with elegance and grace and was always sweet. She didn't have a family and never talked about her life.

You work with a lot of different people. Some people are Chatty Kathy's, and you know their whole life story. Some people say very little. She was part of the second group. One of the other sales ladies said to me one day, ask her what she did for a living years ago. I tried to extract it from her, but she never talked. She was quite exotic looking. She was petite but she carried herself like she was 6 feet tall. Her back was so straight, and she had the most graceful walk. Her skin was flawless. I commented that she had the most beautiful skin I had ever seen. She explained it came from her mother being Asian and her father being Russian.

We became pretty close but still she never talked about anything.

One day a young girl came in looking for shoes. They called on her because she was very knowledgeable. She pulled out several styles of shoes, but nothing pleased this little snit. She became downright rude to her. As she began to assist her, her hand pushed down on one side of her foot.

The young girl said be careful in a very nasty voice. "I'm a ballerina and I need to protect my feet! Don't push down on the side of my foot like that." My friend apologized but she continued on with her rant. "You obviously don't know how to handle special people do you?"

My other sales lady friend said quietly so she couldn't hear her, "My, my now that's a bunion!"

Rose smiled and said, "Forgive me dear."

After she left, Rose took her shoe off and showed me her foot. "Look at these feet. I danced for well over thirty years and they are perfect!"

"You were a dancer, Rose?"

She smiled and said she had danced with the American Ballet Theater Company and was a Prima Ballerina. She continued on. If you visit New York City and go to the American Ballet Theatre you could see me dance on film. She danced with the greats! I will do something I never do Gia. I will bring in some pictures for you to see.

After a while I assumed she forgot so I never brought it up again. One day she carried in a briefcase and asked me to let her know when I would be at lunch. We sat down in a quiet corner, and she pulled out pictures of her dancing at the White House for President and Mrs. Kennedy. She took off her ballet slippers and handed them to Mrs. Kennedy. She explained Mrs. Kennedy said Caroline would love them.

Rose was in her glory. More pictures spilled out of her briefcase, and I don't know what impressed me more. The people that attended the event at the White House or the dancers who you would all know!

Episode 31:

Back to Hell

Okay let's go on back to Cooper and Flux.

Sales were on and off and Christmas was approaching. Mr. Stein had realized that Yori Karamurra had a very special eye for design. He was given the position of window dresser at a very upscale hotel. We had a case there and he did an awesome job displaying our beautiful design pieces. He knew he was good and let everyone know how much business he brought in from the display. He was pompous in his slim cut suits and flamboyant mannerisms.

He was likable but something was not quite right. You couldn't put your finger on it. There was something off. The other ladies were not a fan of his either. Now let me spend a few minutes on Mr. Peepers or Daniel Saltzman. He was somewhat knowledgeable about watches. What he didn't know he would bull shit his way around. Joe was not a fan. He said the same thing I said. He is full of shit! If I didn't know something I would refer to Joe. If Mr. Peepers didn't know something, that was a different story. He was a bull shit artist and not liked by anyone except Mr. Stein and maybe Yori.

It was kind of strange how the two of them became friends. If you work together for a period of time, you get to know people. Mary, the older lady, and I became friends. You would never think it possible. I became friends with pretty much everyone. It was an assortment of quirky, strange, funny people. Some were basically good people. Then there were the others.

They were Mr. Stein's inner sanctum. All were opportunistic types that knew on which side their bread was buttered. They always agreed with him while laughing at him behind his back. It was a pretty sick environment, as I have discussed before. I had earlier discussed the incident involving David Stubl. He worked for the old man for over twenty years. Yet, it was like he disappeared into thin air. Stein never prosecuted him. I could not understand this. Joe said he belonged to the same clubs and knew many of the same people. Poof, you're a thief and now you are gone. I got to be friends with the really older lady GG as well as Rosa and Jax. We were tight just like the back-office people. Yvette, Joe and the regulars. This was our group. Time continued to pass.

After the incident with David Stubl, I made a mental note to myself. I would not get rattled by events that I'm not responsible for. In theory, it's very good but reality is something else.

Julie and Mr. Stein had an extremely wealthy couple that were at one time top clients. They would visit the salon every week and look at so much jewelry that Julie would tell them to take the items home and see how it works with their lifestyle.

They didn't pay at the time. We would make a memo on the item, and they would sign for it. After a while, they would either keep the jewelry or watch or return it. If they decided to keep the item, they would call us, and we would send an invoice.

Something changed in their lifestyle and to put it bluntly, they lost a lot of their wealth. That did not prevent them from coming into the salon. Mr. Stein became tired of their visits. He allowed Julie to take control of their account. Julie, enjoying their company, would spend hours with them. They continued browsing and taking home special pieces. Most of the time the items would be returned. Mr. Stein voiced his annoyance about them. Julie, however, did not care. She chatted away for many hours. One particular visit they selected two expensive sapphire and diamond items. One item was a very lovely ring. The other item was a long chain with alternating diamonds and sapphires. A memo was made on the two pieces.

I want to go on record to state this happened with many clients. They would look at something and then want to take it home to make sure they wanted it. Thus, we would make a personal memo with all the information.

After some time had passed, Mr. Stein asked Julie to check and find out if they were keeping any of the items. About a week later, the lady dropped off the ring at the salon. Yours truly took the ring from her and checked the ring back into stock. I found the memo, circled the item, and wrote it returned to stock. It was only the ring.

I was questioned about this event extensively. I was being interrogated. It reminded me of the TV show Dragnet. The facts lady only the facts.

I couldn't understand what the problem was until Julie said repeatedly, "What did you write down. Could you have mistaken the fact that she had two items with her to return?"

I finally told Julie, "I have already explained to you what happened. She returned one item. It was the ring."

After a few quiet sessions with the boss, she confronted me. "Gia, listen. The client is certain she returned two items, and you received them."

I looked her straight in the eyes and said, "Perhaps she had a few drinks at lunch, and it slipped her mind."

Her expression was as if I had accused her of murder. "The client," she said, "is very well known here. Her reputation is pristine. I think you had better rethink this situation. You do not seem to be concerned about this incident, but your reputation and job are at stake here."

Again, I looked her straight in the eye. Though I was shaking inside, I sternly answered her back with a terse tone in my voice. "I'm not concerned one bit. There is an error here. However, I did not make it."

"We will have to investigate the entire incident."

"Fine." I replied. I left the back room and overheard her say to Mr. Stein that I was an arrogant little bitch. How dare she infer that Lois either forgot or was drunk.

The next couple of weeks went on as usual. I waited for a scene to erupt but nothing happened. During the down time, I would go into the safe and sit down on a chair and pretend I was wiping off some of the old gold pieces of jewelry.

I chanted to myself "Nam Myo Ho Renge Kyo. Please let someone find the missing piece of jewelry."

Julie would throw me a look here and there. One day she said, "Well Miss Nichols anything new going on in your life to report?"

I simply gave her a blank stare and said, "No Julie. Do you have anything to tell me?"

It remained that way for quite a while. I had to tell someone, so I told Mary. She said, "Remember when we lost a piece of jewelry or remember when something disappeared out of our stock? It will turn up. It is either misplaced or someone has it and forgot. I know it's not you. Don't worry." I continued to Chant for an answer.

It seemed an eternity. One day Julie saw me in the safe and simply said, "Oh, I think it slipped my mind, but Lois called about the necklace. She found it."

Rosa told me she transferred the call to Julie. The call had come in ten days earlier. The two women thought it was so funny that the necklace was thrown into a drawer at home. It was a joke at my expense. Rosa said Mr. Stein reprimanded Julie for being so casual about the stock with Lois.

Episode 32:

Unusual Dates

Barbi and I continued our friendship. I continued using the internet dating service.

I met a nice guy, although a little strange. Why am I not surprised? I worked in a strange place—my dating should be strange as well. He was a businessman. He liked very nice things. Like a lot of men I met, he liked to impress me with what he did for a living. Men also liked to impress people with their material possessions. He had a nice personality and was charming in his manner. He was not handsome but that was not an issue. I liked a man who was successful. He was hard working and that was appealing. He never tried to kiss me. I found that rather strange. He said he thought I was beautiful. He kept asking me out.

After about five dates, he made no moves on me. We went on a dinner cruise on Lake Michigan. It was a dressy evening. I wore a black bodysuit. It was sheer with a slightly plunging neckline. I wore a straight to the knee skirt. I had a rule. If the neckline plunged the skirt should be conservative. I finished the outfit with very high heels.

We enjoyed a great dinner. After dinner, we danced. An older gentleman came over and said to me, "I don't want to impose but I can see you are a good dancer. He continued, "I love to dance."

He turned to my date and asked him if he would mind if he borrowed me for a special dance. My date surprised me and said, "Sure, I love to watch great dancing."

He turned to the D.J and asked for an Argentinian Tango. Right out of an old movie the scent of a woman song. (Por Una Cabeza) Off we went. He was an amazing dancer and if I do say so myself, I can follow anyone. My mother was a professional dancer and taught me well.

The music started and the lights dimmed slightly. Everyone cleared the dance floor to watch us. I could feel my face go red. The man whispered to me and said, "Be proud of not only how you look carissima, but how you move!"

I glanced over at my date. He looked at me like I was delectable. Good I thought. Maybe he will try to kiss me tonight? I had not danced with someone who could dance as well as I could for a long time. This was a treat.

After the dance he said, "A quick step? Would you like to waltz?"

"Sorry," I said., "I appreciate this wonderful dance that I thoroughly enjoyed. I cannot leave my date." Apparently, he didn't care about his date. I could not be rude.

"Thank you for the wonderful opportunity to dance this special tango." He bowed to me and tried to hand me his card. Where he had it, I never knew. I shook my head as both of our dates did not look happy. The other people on the floor applauded.

My date asked me, "How can I follow that?"

I said, "You have your own gifts and never compare yourself to others."

He smiled and said, "Thank you. You know exactly what to say to make a man feel special." I was about ready for a major move. He surprised me and took me back to my apartment.

He said, "I'm going out of the country for about six weeks. When I return, I would like to take you shopping for a new car. Your car is falling apart, and I would like to do something special for you."

I never asked for anything from any man. I was shocked at this statement. Also, he didn't want to come up to my apartment. Why would he make this exclamation out of the blue? He shocked me.

I told Barbi about this, and she said, "He has a problem. How long is he going to be gone?" I said, "Six weeks, is what he said."

"Wait, something is strange. No moves on you?"

"No." I said.

"He sees you dance a very sexy dance and nothing?"

"Right." I said.

"Hmmm. Something is up and I don't mean his cock." We laughed. The next day was work and I did not think about him.

Sales went up and sales went down. The jewelry business is very strange. Sometimes, people are shopping and other days just nothing. I kept on with my dating sites. Good entertainment but that was about it. One night I saw an email from an older man. I almost hit the delete button, because of his age. There was something about him that was endearing. I decided to give him my phone number and we talked for about an hour. He turned out to be of Greek heritage like me. We had so much in common. Again, the usual story. Let's see how we can impress each other. He told me yadda, yadda, yadda. After our fifth conversation on the phone, I thought he was safe. He was appealing because we were two Greek people and there is a common bond, when you have your family's ethnicity in common.

I asked him, "Would you like to meet for a drink and more conversation?"

He said, "That would be fantastic. Unfortunately, I cannot drive. I'm having surgery in a few days for a knee replacement, and I can't drive. How about I send a car for you, and we go to a nice restaurant out here." He lived in one of the ritziest neighborhoods on the North Shore. Remembering what I was told by Barbi and the book she gave me, this was a big NO. NO!

I told Barbi and she said, "Tell him YOU DON'T DELIVER the goods!"

I said, "What!?" She said it again. "I said that's rude, don't you think."

She said, "Weed out the jerks and give him a difficult time, because men like that. They like a challenge. It is the caveman syndrome. They like fighting for you because they feel they have to work for good things."

I wasn't going to say this, but she was right about so many things. I got the nerve and said that to him. He listened, there was silence at the other end and then laughter like I've never heard before. A big laugh and he repeated what I said. He had a low, sexy voice for an older man. He laughed like Santa Claus. A huge belly laugh.

"Ok Gia, I will call you back in a while after the surgery and I am well." I felt a bit sad because I liked his personality.

Thinking I would never hear from him again I hung up.

Episode 33:

Super Strange People

Work continued to progress. One day an interesting lady walked into the store. It was cold outside, and she was wearing a mink coat. She was a little plump and wore stiletto high heels. She asked to see the boss. I went into the back and asked Mr. Stein if he would please come out for a client.

He said the usual. "What's her name? Do you know her? Do I know her? Ok put her into a small office."

He then calls Joe Brickmann to wait on her. He couldn't be bothered with people he didn't know. Joe went into the office and about three minutes later he said to Mr. Stein "She wants you."

He said, "Tough shit. I don't know this person. I don't want to be bothered."

Joe said, "I think you better see this one." He puts a mint in his mouth (good thing) and goes into the office.

Her name is Tisa, and she has a thick accent. She told Stein she would be coming back tomorrow with a friend, and she wants only him to wait on them. He's a doctor, an older gentleman and he's extremely rich.

"I want you to show him only expensive things," she continued. "You will be glad to make his acquaintance." He was so sweet butter would have melted in his mouth. His personality changed from not caring, to one of very interested. I wanted to puke at his suave demeanor.

He said goodbye and came into the back room. We were all watching on the monitor. He said, "What do you think about her, Julie?"

"About what Bern?"

"Didn't you see her?"

"Sure." she said.

"She probably is a hooker, and this is her John."

"Geeze, Bern, I don't know!"

"See if she even shows up!"

The next day at the appointed time she reserved bingo and a big Limousine pulled up in front of the store. Out of the car comes the same lady of the day before, wearing the same mink coat. She is followed by a short pudgy old geezer! It looks like old Julie was right. He looked like a man of some importance. We put them in the big office Mr. Stein used for his special clients only. After that, I went into the back with everyone else to watch the monitor.

Ten minutes later a very excited Bernard Stein comes into the back and hands me a tray he was holding. He told me to get him rings and bracelets up to seventy-five thousand dollars. He then yells for Julie and gives her the 411 on the doctor. He asked her to help him, and he told me to assist Julie. The foam was all over his lips and Julie told him in her twang to wipe his mouth. Galy yells to Mr. Stein not to go back into that room right now. There is a show going on in your office. I don't exactly remember who was where because pandemonium broke out. People were pushing people to get a view of the show.

Mr. Stein asked Julie what to do? Julie says knock first. Tisa was working the doctor over and according to the monitor, she was successful. The woman started flashing her coat open to reveal a totally nude, good shaped older lady! She was singing a foreign song. I think it was German and he was buying what she was selling! Dancing around the room and moving her legs provocatively. It was steamy!

Joe yelled down to Stein. "I would wait if I were you. The sale might be larger."

Meanwhile, I'm pulling a lot of merchandise for Julie. Everyone started laughing and we were pushing each other out of the way to get a better view. After she closed her coat and sat herself down, Joe yelled down to tell the boss that he can go in now.

Galy says, "What is this a threesome!?"

I don't know what was funnier the show in the office or the crazy salespeople watching the show.

He spent $65,000 on a beautiful diamond rope that was about 20 inches in length. We ran the credit card, ka-ching, ka-ching.

Tisa tells Mr. Stein she would call him next week and set up another appointment. "Please have chilled champagne ready to go." Mr. Stein gives Tisa a kiss and shakes the doctor's hand and bye-bye.

"That was quite a show!" Galy announced.

Joe comes running down the stairs and asks if we should get some vendors in line? He was told, "If she asks for something specific, we can move then and get things in within a day or so."

Then he turned and said to everyone in earshot. "Thank you for assisting me in this unique sale."

Galy said, "Good thing our police couldn't see what was going on or you might have been arrested for permitting a lewd show."

He told Galy, "Leave the humor at your desk please."

Episode 34:

The Gentleman from Asia Returns

It was about two weeks later or so when I got a phone call from the mysterious disappearing man. It sounded like he was far away. His voice was trailing off a bit. He sounded weak and hoarse. In fact, he sounded very sad. We had some very nice dates, and he was always a gentleman. Just hearing his voice, I knew something was wrong.

After he asked me how I was doing, he started his story. He had gone to China. He had a procedure of some sort. It did not go well, and he was going to go somewhere in Texas to try and have it fixed. He didn't really explain too much. I felt very sorry for him. He was a nice man. Somehow, I felt I wouldn't be hearing from him again.

I thought about it and surmised that because he never made a move on me, he had a sexual operation that failed and now was totally messed up. I mentioned it to my girlfriend Barbi, and she agreed with me. She and I thought he was impotent and had gone to China to have a rod put in. The results were not what he wanted. Why would you go to China of all places? I know he did business over there. It still didn't make sense. The whole story was so convoluted. I thought a lot about our last conversation and was very sorry for him. He mentioned he had some kind of surgery that was supposed to fix his slight problem. He had some kind of infection which made his condition worse. He said to give him some time and he would contact me again with an update.

I didn't think I would hear back from him.

I did not.

Episode 35:

More Fun with Interesting People

Work went on as usual. I was having issues with Mr. Peepers, who was always trying to put in his two senses when I was trying to sell a watch. Joe told me that if I had an issue to call him in and I could tell him to mind his own business. Of course, the boss liked him, which made everything more difficult. He also tried to push Judy around. She was a really nice girl, and we were invited to her home for a birthday party for her toddler son. She was an animal lover as I was, and her personality was so funny and sweet. Her husband was a nice sort of guy. I never really hung out with them. Married people had their own type of life. In our environment at work we were friendly. There was a lot of downtime in the jewelry business, and you got to know a lot about the people you worked with.

It took a couple more weeks and we were heavy into the Christmas season. A call came in from our former interesting client Tisa. She wanted to come in on a weekday to see Mr. Stein. He was glad because many of his regulars came in on Saturday. We were ready with the champagne, and no one took lunch that day. We wanted to see what kind of show would take place. Even Julie was trying to speculate what would happen.

In the morning, a very big client of Mr. Stein's came in with his scarecrow girlfriend. She was always decent to me and only asked for me. They lived together in a magnificent penthouse apartment on East Lake Shore Drive. That day he bought her an amazing diamond necklace for $150,000. They were going to a charity event, and she had nothing to wear.

I found out years later that she would refer to me as her shop girl. Sometimes you perceive people to be ordinary nice people and then you find out they looked down at you. It makes a person feel sad. She was jealous of my friend Yvette. It seemed the scarecrow's friend was once married to the man who was now dating Yvette. The scarecrow and her friend were both gold diggers. She made nasty comments to Mr. Stein about Yvette. I think she wanted to get her fired. She was saying disparaging things. Mr. Stein listened and said nothing to Yvette. You see, Yvette's new boyfriend was a very nice man and really liked her. He was a very wealthy man. He realized his former wife was only after his money, so he dumped her.

One day, he came in for a repair on his watch and Mr. Peepers was busy, so Yvette stepped in. They immediately hit it off and started dating. Yvette fell hard. We were all hoping something nice would happen for her because she had a difficult life. She had been married to a wealthy car dealer. She lived in a gorgeous apartment on Lake Shore Drive and was a customer at our salon. From what I know, she was always a doll and was kind and never haughty. She treated everyone like they mattered. Her husband got into drugs and lost everything. Our lives were very similar. I was married to a car dealer who had the same problem.

Getting back to beautiful Yvette. She was ten years older than me. Tiny with jet black hair. She always wore perfect makeup and she dressed impeccably. It was no wonder he fell for her. He was married to a bitch who led him around by the nose. He got out of that miserable marriage and stumbled upon Yvette. They were a couple. Anyway, the scarecrow was not successful. We were happy for her. Mr. Stein was so happy that he made a nice sale. He was hoping Tisa would not disappoint him. We all waited.

Episode 36:

The Show of All Shows

At about two o'clock, a limousine pulled up again and out jumped Tisa. The pudgy old doctor followed her, and the security guards were not paying too much attention. The Dr. went around to the other door and helped someone else out of the car. The most gorgeous young girl stepped out of the car. Everyone in the salon turned their necks to get a glimpse of this amazing girl. She was no more than eighteen or nineteen years old. Okay, I'm not good at telling age. She was at the most twenty years old.

She was about five-foot-seven inches tall. She was a size 2 or 4. A mane of golden blonde hair cascaded down her back. She had big blue eyes and long black lashes. She wore no makeup except a little lip gloss. She looked like an angel but could have been a model. There was an innocence about her. One could not stop staring at her! She wore a simple black straight skirt, a crisp white blouse and high heels. We had seen many beautiful women walk into the salon. This girl was in the top 10 percent. The security guards, who usually show no emotion, wanted to lie down on the floor so she wouldn't dirty her feet!

"Let her walk on me so she doesn't soil herself." Dave whispered to me.

I escorted the party into the large office and informed Mr. Stein they were in the room he had set aside for them. He asked me. "Nichols who is the second woman?"

"Mr. Stein, they didn't introduce her to me, but she is a dream"! Everyone in the back office jumped to the monitors to get a glimpse. Mr. Stein, who never said anything, let out a low whistle. "Wait until you see her face." I said.

He turned to me and said bring down the champagne. Popping a mint into his mouth and straightening his tie, he presented himself to the group. After the niceties, he came back to us. Dazed, he said bring out the best we have. First rings, next bracelets and then necklaces. They stayed for over an hour looking at everything we had.

Stein came back in. He announced they had not decided! He was depressed. Julie told him to leave them alone for a while. You are right on top of them. Leave them with three of the most expensive things you have shown them and let them alone. We were all holding our breath waiting. All of a sudden, Tisa left to use the bathroom.

The young girl gently kissed the old geezer's head. She then took his hand and guided it up her skirt. She wiggled in the chair and her blouse was suddenly showing two pert breasts. No bra was holding them up. It was just her and her nipples. The gyrating continued. His face became very red, and he took his time exploring under her skirt. She dipped her finger in the champagne and then put it in her mouth pursing her lips. Her finger traveled in and out of her mouth. She was NOT an angel! He thought she was though. He started to drool.

She threw her head back and moaned. We heard the moan in the back and the visual was not sensual. If he was about thirty years old and handsome you would call it excellent porn. She took her finger out of her mouth and touched him. He encouraged her to explore him, and she obliged. I was grateful he did not undress.

The office was becoming messy with Dr. Pudgy and Angel getting acquainted in a very personal way. The monitors in the back were becoming steamy from all the salespeople. Everyone was pushing each other to get a better look. There were three large security cameras in the office they were in. The doctor did not care. For an old man he was very active. Moving here and there, he was a very busy man! He said something to her, and she threw her head back. She laughed and continued her act. Her breasts spilled out of the blouse, and she did not care! He was trying to get down on his knees, but he was chunky and there was no room.

After a few minutes more Tisa knocked on the door. There was chatter and then they looked like they wanted the old man back. Julie told Mr. Stein to go back into the office. He stepped back into the office and they exchanged words.

He turned on his heels and said to me, "Get me a six-carat diamond bracelet quickly." He went back for more talk.

He came back again and yelled out to Joe. "Do we have any rope up there?"

"What?"

"Rope, Joe. Rope!"

"For what?"

"Never mind find it!"

Joe looked everywhere, as he called out to everyone." Do we have any rope?" Everyone was too busy watching the monitors and were upset that they were brought into the picture.

Stein told Joe, "They want to tie the doctor up in the limo!"

"We have no rope Mr. Stein."

"Oh shit!" he yelled. He never swore, or hardly ever anyway.

"What are they buying?" Joe asked.

"All the large things I have shown them!"

"Give them your tie Bern!"

"What? This is Hermés!"

Joe said, "How much is the sale?"

He turned to Myron and told him to add this up quickly. He added don't make any mistakes! Right in the middle of this entire exchange Mrs. Stein called. She wanted to talk to her husband. He grabs the phone.

"Honey, I can't talk right now." He gives her a short synopsis of what is going on and he hands the phone to Galy. "Tell her I have to go back into the office."

Mrs. Stein told Galy, "Tell Bern to wash his hands twice before he comes home."

Well, gentle reader, everyone left happy. They spent $325,000. The items purchased were as follows, diamond necklace, two bracelets, (one smaller one for Tisa) and an exquisite diamond ring. Don't forget they also received one Hermés tie! No charge.

We thought the earlier morning sale was excellent. No one said anything at first. It was quiet. I think we all needed to process the entire scenario. Clapping, laughing and congratulations to Mr. Stein went around the office! He then casually announced, "This episode stays here. No one had better say anything. You know, if I hear, heads will roll."

The young woman's name was Krystal Kaye. He wanted the receipt written out in her name. They did not visit a lot. They did revisit. Whenever they did, the security guards would be much more alert! Obviously not because they were fearful but because no one could take their eyes off beautiful Krystal.

Occasionally, she would stop in for a jewelry cleaning. I had the pleasure of taking in her jewelry. Interestingly, whenever she would take off her rings for cleaning, she would put her finger in her mouth to moisten it with saliva. I quickly would pick up a tray so as not to have to touch anyone who did this. It was rather gross. I wondered why people thought that it was necessary when Windex works the best. It makes the muscles contract, and the rings slide right off. It also looks a hell of a lot better!

"Do a lot of wealthy older men visit the special jewelry salons?"

"You are wondering?"

"Of course!"

"Very rich men with not very attractive faces are regulars. They have one thing in common: a pocket personality! Young beautiful girls who just want money will do anything to get it. Many gold diggers visit often."

A friend of mine used to share her escapades of when she was young and beautiful. A lot of times I would have to say stop. When I knew where she was going with her story. I never knew women would do so many weird things. She told me about one man we both knew who loved golden showers. She would have to sit on a ladder. I had to repeat to her to stop. That is too much information. So many stories would make you throw up!

Episode 37:

Work Continues.
Dating as Well.

Work was very busy for two weeks before the holiday.

Everyone was glad when the Christmas season was over. Also, it meant bonus time! My check increased about $1,500.00 for that Christmas. After all the years I had been there, I expected more.

If you think that was a lot, it wasn't. If you were on commission. A check for at least $10,000 would be normal. He always made a big deal about it. The people that had been in the business knew that with commission, the sky's the limit. If you were a good salesperson, you did very well.

It was a bit after the holiday when I finally heard from my friend that had gone to China for surgery. I guess wherever he went, the surgery could not be corrected and so he was the way he was. He never did explain it to me, but I knew. He sent me a couple dozen red roses and the card was sweet but very sad.

My Greek friend called me. His surgery on his knee went well. He asked, "Could we now meet for dinner?"

I said to him, "How about a drink first and see if we like each other?"

"Oh I know I'm going to like you," he said, "but ok. What kind of wine do you like?"

"I like all kinds." I said.

"Specifically." he answered back.

"I don't know much about wine." I answered.

He said his favorite was a wine called Chateau Margaux. "Oh," I answered, "I know that is very expensive. My ex used to drink a wine called Chateau Lafite Rothschild 1982." To me it was all the same.

He started laughing. "Well let's see if I have a bottle somewhere."

"Oh no." I answered. "I didn't tell you to bring me anything."

He continued to laugh that deep Santa Claus-like laugh. He told me he had a slight limp from the surgery. He hoped it wouldn't bother me? I wanted to tell him that the last man I dated had a bigger problem than a slight limp but of course I didn't.

We met a couple days later, and he greeted me at the bar with a couple dozen roses and of course the bottle of wine we discussed. He told me he had lost his wife about six months ago. He was very lonely. He also had a brochure of several vacation places, and he told me to pick a place I would like to go to and visit.

I laughed and said, "I would love to go to Greece."

"This is not the right time of year. We could go somewhere very nice. Of course there would be separate bedrooms," he said.

I laughed this time and said, "Sure. If you are trying to impress me, you are overdoing it a bit."

"Listen, honey, I know how to impress. This is nothing."

I took the wine and the roses. We did have dinner too and it was delicious. Thank you, Nick. What else would a Greek be named LOL. It was either Nick, George or Gus.

He asked me if he could use my bathroom as he had diabetes and was afraid the ride home might be a bit long. Here it comes, I thought.

He read my mind and said, "I promise no moves. Besides, you could outrun me."

"Listen, my apartment is very small," I said. "They have a bathroom at the restaurant. We could just walk back."

"Come on," Nick said, "I am a gentleman."

Barbi would have slapped me square in the face. I felt sorry for him. "Okay," I said, "but remember it's a small place."

Upstairs we went. He walked into my apartment and headed into the bathroom. When he came out, he said, "I see you have a couple dozen roses in your bathroom. I'm not the only one chasing you." He said with his twinkling eyes. "You don't like him much, do you?"

"What makes you say that?"

"Why would you put them in the bathroom?"

"No reason." I said. In truth, I had very little extra space to put anything.

He stood in my living room and glanced around. He then walked into my bedroom and gave it the once over as well. I knew he was very wealthy. I refused to be intimidated.

He looked at me and said, "You know Gia, you live in a dump!"

"Excuse me?" I said. "That is not a nice thing to say to someone you supposedly want to date."

Laughing again, he said, "I have to get you out of here."

"Okay Nick, You did not score any points with your criticism."

He kissed me gently and said, "I will call you. Have a look at the brochures. Also, enjoy the wine."

"Thank you," I said.

Then my son came home. Good thing he wasn't there when Nick came up.

He saw the wine and said, "Mom, who gave you this?"

"The man I met on People match."

"Do you know how expensive it is!?"

"No, should I know?"

"Tomorrow I will call a liquor store and ask. I think you will be surprised."

Episode 38:

Nick Continues the Hot Pursuit

The next day, Nick called. "Well did you have a look at the brochures?" he asked.

"No." I said.

"Why not? This is not acceptable."

"Because you are rushing me."

"Is that bad?"

"No, but let's have a few dates first please!"

"Ha! Ha!" More chuckles. "Listen, why don't you come over to my house on Saturday, and we can go to dinner, and I can show you my art!"

"Very funny." I said.

"Bring a girlfriend with you," he offered. "I'm not the type to take advantage of anyone."

Barbi was busy but very intrigued by what he had to say. I did not mention he told me I lived in a dump, because I didn't think it was very nice. I instead asked my girlfriend Gina. She lived in Buffalo Grove, and she could drive over to Barrington. I told her to be on time. I trusted him but you can't be too careful.

The limousine picked me up after work. I borrowed some jewelry from work. That was no problem because the boss always liked to show off his jewelry. The only thing, if we got held up, I would be responsible for it. I don't usually wear anything out because I couldn't afford to pay for its replacement. In this case, I felt safe enough. I chose a beautiful Henry Dunay 18Kt and diamond watch. I also wore a necklace that was quite pretty. I really loved the Dunay watch and wore it in the store often.

The ride from the city was long. Gina called and had a difficult time finding the area. "Geeze Gia, did you know how big the houses are out here?" she said.

"No, I don't know. I have never been there."

"They are estates on quite a few acres." she exclaimed!

"Please Gina don't be late. I don't want to get into trouble." I exclaimed.

I was wondering if I was dressed well enough. I wore my usual little black dress. Oh well I thought he knew I wasn't rich.

The driveway was about two miles long and winding along this Asian type of garden. The house was immense. Gina was waiting for me in the driveway with her lights off. She couldn't speak.

"Who is this guy?" she asked me in Greek.

"I met him on the dating site. He's Greek."

"Who cares!" she shot back.

Wow! If the inside is anything like the outside. I think I'm in another world! We rang the doorbell. He was casually dressed. I was overdressed. He had on khaki slacks and gym shoes.

"You look very nice." he said.

I introduced him to Gina. He liked her. Gina was gorgeous! She was married so there is no competition. She is tall and very exotic looking. She wore jeans and boots with a sweater. Her hair was long, and she had very exotic features. She had a Roman nose, but it suited her. Her face was a combination of Angelina Jolie and Sophia Loren. Also, she had full lips and high cheekbones. She was beautiful inside, more importantly. A kinder person I had never known.

Let's get back to the estate. A huge double door with an Asian motif carved in the entrance greeted us. The entry hall had a waterfall right opposite the front door. Oriental music was piped into the sound system. Nick had put some sort of kimono over his usual khakis with gym shoes on. The house was about 20,000 square feet with two kitchens. It also had a guest house. The long hall connected the bedrooms and living room. There was a beautiful atrium in the middle with sky lights everywhere. Chihuly glass were prominent accents. In the main house there were six bedrooms. Just off his bedroom was an Olympic indoor swimming pool. The wall surrounding the pool was all glass. On a nice day you pushed a button, and the glass doors opened and the roof over the pool rolled back. In the hallway that was the atrium, there was a silver eagle that was suspended from the ceiling and looked as if it was suspended in flight. It was over fifteen feet long. The living room went on forever. Connected to the living room was a long hallway. This connected to his bedroom. His bathroom, connected to her bathroom. There was a sunken tub on a high platform. To the right of the tub was a Balinese shower. Now you might wonder what that is? It's a shower that is completely open. No shower doors or curtains. It had two large water heads. It resembled rain and it had various strengths you could set. In his bathroom, he had a steam shower that was malachite and onyx. There were African frescos everywhere. He also had a collection of Asian artifacts. Connected to the main kitchen was a hot house filled with all types of orchids. You name it, he had it! On the wall was another beautiful Kimono encased in glass. He said he wore it for parties. He gave me a price tag of $100,000 for it. Let's go back to his bedroom now. Connected to his bedroom was a closet that was also glass and was its own room. Connected to the closet was a safe room. He also had a computer room that had four different computers. I had to hold on to my girlfriend because I had never seen a home like this! The garage was in the basement that you drove into. It had room for ten cars. I told him this is really cool but what do you do in the winter? It's heated everywhere. Snow doesn't stick around too much.

He laughed that Santa Claus laugh of his. My girlfriend turned to me and asked in Greek, "Is he for real?" I gave her a look like a truck had just hit me.

He took us into his safe room.

"Gia, here is where my wife kept her jewelry. My

daughter has taken most of it out. You will meet her in a couple of weeks. Have you decided where you want to go for a vacation?"

I looked at him and said, "No, I haven't looked."

"Well get on it. I like to travel. You will need some clothes," and he reached into the safe and took out cash that was banded and it said $5,000.00.

I looked at him and said, "I cannot take that Nick."

"It's not enough? Take two." he replied.

"No, I can't take one." I said. I finally said, "Listen this is a lot to digest all at once."

He laughed. "Let's go to dinner. Please come with us Gina."

"No," she said, "my family is waiting for me, and I have to lie down, because I feel a headache developing."

"Call them and have them meet us wherever you would like to go."

"Thank you, Nick, but it's a pass for now."

We went under the house to the garage, and he asked, "Which car should we take?"

We ended up taking a beautiful Ferrari. We drove a short distance and ended up at a steakhouse. Everyone knew him. We were seated and he asked me what I felt like eating.

"Do you think they might have fish?" I meekly asked. It was the first real sentence I was able to speak since seeing his house.

"If they don't, we will go somewhere else."

The head waiter heard me and said, "Madam, just tell me what you feel like eating and we will get it and make it for you." I had Dover Sole, and it was delicious!

During dinner he told me all about himself. He told me his story. I will not get into the details. If I ever wanted to protect a person's identity it is his. Remember kind reader, this is not fiction. A friend of Barbi's heard about Nick from her and tried to contact him. How she found his profile, I do not know. He told me someone tried to contact him, and he said to her, please do not bother to contact me again. I'm not interested.

"You know Gia, I'm not interested in gold diggers. You are the real deal, and I like you."

I could name five women that would do the exact same thing. He was a genuine guy! He didn't have to prove anything like so many men I had seen and dated. He was indeed a genius in certain areas. He built quite a few companies. He was extremely successful world-wide. His mathematical skills were unbelievable. Besides being incredibly brilliant, he was also street smart. He could size up people and businesses in record time. Also, he was humble and charitable. In short, I've never met a man like him.

After dinner, he handed me more brochures. "I'm giving you these again. Kindly do your homework." He then picked up his phone and said, "I will call my driver to take you home."

He called me as I was walking into my apartment. "I just wanted to make sure you got home okay."

I thought to myself, I know he's not a phony, but he has no filter on his thoughts. Whatever he is thinking just pops right out of his mouth.

"Gia, I know I overwhelmed you and your girl-friend Gina. Hey, are you related?"

"No," I said, "we are very good friends."

"Tell her she is lovely as you are. I enjoyed meeting her. I hope we can all get together soon."

"I will tell her what you said. Nick, I don't know what to say to you. We move in very different circles..."

He interrupted me and said, "Do not say another word. I like you. You are a sincere nice lady. You are also beautiful. Let's see how it goes with us. I will call you in a couple days. Remember to pick a place you want to visit. We will not go by private jet but first class. I use private jets going around the states but not overseas. Unless I need to be on a tight schedule this is my method of travel. I had a good time with you and your friend, and I hope you did as well. Let's not wait too long to see each other again. Bye…"

I went home and looked over the brochures. England, Italy, Spain, France. The brochures all showcased amazing properties. Transportation was private limousine. I've not seen things like this since I was married.

Episode 39:

Trying to Concentrate On Work

The next day I had a difficult time concentrating on work. One of my regulars came in and bought a watch. She was drunk. I knew there was a fifty-fifty chance that she would sober up and decide if she would keep it. She could afford it. She was in a mood. Whenever she would have dealings with her ex-husband, and this was her third or fourth (I lost count), she would come in and always buy something. The next day after she was somewhat sober, she would either keep it or bring it back. She was a miserable person. The woman never smiled. While she was looking at the watches, there was a lady looking at watches with Mr. Peepers. She walked over and said, "Move over, I'm looking too." She then gave her a shove.

I walked in the back and reported the incident to Mr. Stein. Since he knew her and her family quite well.

"Who is the woman she shoved? Do we know her?"

"Mr. Peepers said she was a walk-in." I swear that creepy kid was everywhere. He was always listening.

"Leave it alone," he said, "unless she gets nasty."

"Shoving a nice lady is unacceptable." I repeated.

"Leave it Nichols." he replied.

I went back out and she saw my Henry Dunay watch. Actually, it wasn't mine, but I was going to save up for it.

"Does that belong to you or the store?" she asked.

"Oh it's the store's." I replied.

"I didn't think you could afford it," she chuckled. "I thought it belonged to the store. No, It's too dressy" she said and continued looking.

Nice little slap, but I was used to it.

Well the next day the watch she purchased was not returned. She bought a Cartier tank watch on a strap. The Cartier watch she originally wanted was showing in our inventory, but I couldn't find it. I asked Rosa and she said she checked in a couple like that so I should find it. I asked everyone, GG was busy too. She was waiting on one of her regulars. She was a spoiled brat, who had just gotten a divorce. Lucky her, her parents had money. So it didn't matter. Mr. Peepers was huddled in a corner with Yori. Lately the two have become frenemies. They never were friends. Lately they seemed to have found a new relationship. Joe was not a fan of either one. He wouldn't say anything about Yori. I knew he didn't like Daniel (Mr. Peepers.). He pretended to know much more than he did. All in all, it was a busy day. I didn't find the watch. I looked for something else.

The following day was mildly busy. Mary and Yvette both had sales. Judy had a sale too. The old man was his usual pain in the ass. 'Who is it? Do we know them? What do they want? If you didn't make a sale, don't forget to put it in the book so we know. What did you do wrong? Why didn't they purchase?' It got so everyone would make up something. Some people just come in to browse. I was thinking about my time there and seven years had gone by in a flash. It seemed like yesterday. Yvette and her boyfriend were moving into a very nice condo together. The talk continued in the back about the two of them. Of course, it continued when she was not around. She decided to only work part time. The old man was not happy about it. When it was our day off, or when we were at lunch it was gossip time.

I got a call a few days later. It was a lady that wanted to make an appointment with me. After we just about finished, she dropped her father's name (It was Greek Nick).

He and I had a very nice dinner together the night before. He pushed me about the trip. Again, he made it clear wherever we stayed, we would have a suite with two bedrooms. I said I would consider the UK. I hadn't been there in a long time, and it seemed appealing.

"Good for you." Barbi said. "I never thought little Miss Goody Two Shoes would ever consider a trip with an older man."

So that is where we left it. In fact, he was so sweet and so smart I would have dated him if there was no trip involved.

Now I met his daughter who was a sweet girl. You would never know. Some people have a little money and treat you like a servant. Others that are really wealthy talk to you like an equal. People are interesting, that's for sure.

Her name was Natalie, and she was looking for a necklace for an event. She picked out a very pretty diamond drop necklace with diamonds all around like a tennis necklace. Her price was $40,000. I got the third degree as usual. Who is this person? Do we know her? Has she bought from us before?

"I know her." I answered. "No, she has not purchased here before. She will again."

"How is she paying?"

"I think they will be paying by check. Her father will give me a check tomorrow."

"You mean you want me to release this necklace without payment? Will you stand good for her?"

"Yes." I said. "She will not take it with her. She wants her father to see it."

"Are you serious?"

"Yes." I replied.

"Is she paying tax or are we shipping?"

"He will pay the tax tomorrow."

"Do you know this person?

"Again, I said yes! She will leave the necklace so I may show her father."

"Okay." Myron threw me a look. "Nichols, it would take you a long time to pay this off." he said.

"Don't worry about it. I won't be doing that."

I wrapped it and off she went. She left the necklace with me. The next day we had a snow storm, so I didn't expect him to come to the store. I was reminded by three people.

"Look," I said, "I will stand by him, and I mean it." This is the end of our conversation. I was a bit nervous. At about 4:00pm I had not heard from him, so I assumed the weather had prevented him from coming into the store.

Barbi called me nuts. I believed he was an honorable man. Hell, I saw his house!

It was 4:30pm and the boss gave me a look. One of the security guards came in the back where we were discussing the whole matter and said, "Gia, there is a vagrant asking for you. Should I throw him out?" Everyone runs over to the monitor.

Mr. Stein says, "There is your millionaire now, Gia." Everyone was laughing at his joke. I looked up and it was Nick. I did not say anything to them but told the security guard to put him in a diamond office. I got my sales book, put lipstick on and grabbed the package.

I went through the security doors and said, "Hi Nick."

He apologized for being late. "No problem," I said.

He truly looked a little disheveled. I chuckled to myself. He was wearing his usual outfit. He added a bomber jacket that was slightly soiled. He also added a skull cap. It kind of stuck up like it was just grazing the top of his head. We went into the office. I could imagine what was going on in the back room.

People were casually and purposely walking by. I got up and closed the door.

We had a nice chat. He asked me if I would have dinner tonight. I said, "Well it's not so nice outside."

He said, "That's why we should do dinner HA, HA, HA."

"Okay, sure I said. I opened the package and we both gazed at Natalie's choice.

I guess it's nice he said. I'm not a jewelry person. Natalie is and my late wife was. See this watch. It's a Timex. Ha, Ha, Ha. I called the travel agent, and we would talk about it at dinner.

He took out a checkbook and wrote the check including tax. I went into the back and handed it to Myron and Mr. Stein said to call the bank, "Let's make sure he has funds of some kind."

I went back out and handed the wrapped package to Nick. He said, "I hope they call the bank. Ha, Ha."

"Why? I asked.

"I own the bank.

I walked back and announced to the back office I would be leaving early this evening.

Eight pairs of eyes gave me a look. Who knows what was said but I knew one of my friends would tell me.

We had a great dinner at The Place. There was no splitting anything. We had wine, appetizers and our entree. We also discussed the side trips we would be taking in London. I could choose anything I wanted. He wanted to attend the theater every night we were there.

I told him GREAT! I love the theater. We can go shopping at Knightsbridge and Harrods. I agreed.

"When can you go?" he said.

"I have to ask the boss. Can I let you know tomorrow?"

"Sure, everything can be changed. How long can you be gone?"

"I don't know. I have to check."

"Try for ten days. If you have to do a week, that's fine too. By the way, do you like cruising?"

"I haven't been on a cruise in a long time."

"My wife booked a cruise. She had something happen and she couldn't go. It was $60,000. I have to take it by June 30th of this coming year. Maybe you should request the time now to make sure you can go. I'd hate to lose the money."

He was acting like he wanted this to be a long relationship! I was walking on air. I danced in through the front door of my apartment. I announced to my son the plans we had made. He was flabbergasted!

"Really mom?"

"Yes." I answered. "The only thing is if the old man will give me the time off. You know how he hates people taking vacations."

The next day, I walked into work, and everyone wanted to know who my mystery man was. I mean all my friends asked. The people in the back wanted to ask also but no one did!

Mary told me, "Good thing you left because there were plenty of remarks going back and forth. They looked him up on the Internet. Wow! He owns the bank the check was drawn on!"

"I know." I said.

"Do you know how many companies he owns?"

"No, I just know he is really smart."

She hugged me and then said, "People like you deserve nice things, because you are a real person. There is no phony shit about you! Do you know how many gold diggers would line up to be in your position?"

I guess plenty. I've seen my share of them. (I knew one for sure) I remembered that friend of Barbi's who tried to entice him into taking her out.

Mary was such a kind soul and so was GG. The boss treated Mary ok. He was mean to GG and always spoke condescending to her. Her clients all loved her. If he saw any of her clients out at night wearing the item they purchased from her, he would say you have the best sales lady. We all think highly of her. To her face he made shit out of her. Years passed so quickly. I lost count of how long I had been there. I decided some of the sales force were getting on in life and he had better add to his stable of mules. Throughout my time there he added and subtracted salespeople. I went to my boss a couple days later and asked him about my vacation time.

"Now is not a good time, Nichols. I can't be bothered with it. Ask me in a couple weeks."

I summoned up my courage and said, "That will not work Mr. Stein. My friend wants to take me to London for 10 days, in a couple of weeks. Also in early summer, I will need a couple weeks off for a cruise."

He hit the ceiling. "Listen," I said. "I have not taken a vacation day off in a year and I am entitled to it. He is spending a lot on these trips, and I want to go. His daughter already had spent a great deal of money on that diamond necklace and if you want more business out of that family and the people that work for him, I suggest you give me the time. He also knows a lot of the right people and can recommend Cooper and Flux for their special gifts. His friends are all extremely wealthy. In fact some are on television."

"Who?" he asked and immediately spewed saliva in my face.

"I'm not at liberty to talk about them." I said. "Just know he's not a nobody!"

"I will think about it." He raised his voice.

"I need an answer by tomorrow so I can tell him."

"Okay." He said.

"What?" I repeated.

"Okay. I will let you know tomorrow."

The next day he avoided me like the plague. Finally, at 4:00pm I said in front of the whole back office. "Mr. Stein, you have been avoiding my question and I need an answer today." He tried to make a feeble excuse, but I pressed on. "I need to know today."

Finally, he turned to me with his face red as a beet and said, "Make sure, if you have any pending sales, you make us all aware of them. I don't want any slip ups Nichols. Okay, go then. Give Vasha the dates."

Knowing I had the time off was a relief. Now, did I really want to go?

I spoke with Nick that night. He was so thoughtful. I thought this man is a doll or he is one hundred percent full of shit. The first trip was to London, and it was the queen's 75th birthday. There would be all kinds of things happening in the UK. He asked me about renting a limousine and driver. He wanted to visit Oxford and the Cotswolds. I had never been to the Cotswold area but heard it was lovely. He also said he would set up going to the theater every evening. He would also arrange for high tea and a lot of shopping.

He mentioned a few well known five-star hotels and told me to pick one. I will get two bedrooms and that way you can be comfortable.

"Do you want some money before we leave so you can buy a few things?"

"No." I thanked him but said I was good. "You pick the hotel or have the travel agent suggest a hotel," I said. "It's been a while since I've been to London, and I'd rather not make the wrong choice."

The next few days we were moderately busy at work. I took the opportunity to mentally start packing. I knew Nick NEVER dressed up, but I thought I had better take two dresses that could be considered a step above casual.

I went out for dinner with Barbi and of course we went to our favorite restaurant, The Place. We saw a lot of people and clients from work. Also, two tables away was the old full of crap boss himself with a small party of favorite clients and of course his beloved wife. I had waited on a lot of people in my time, but never as fake as the two of them. They turned on the charm when they wanted. I could just hear me as being the topic of conversation at their table. No one could gossip as well as the two of them.

I turned my attention to Barbi and what was going on in her life.

"Do you remember a year or so ago the guy I dated that looked like Bill Clinton?"

I thought about it for a while. "You know, it's hard to remember all of your dates. Wait a minute, he's the one that chased you around your apartment naked?"

"Gosh Gia, you remember a lot. I wish you could remember for me all the guys that have danced through my life."

"I think it was more like two years or maybe a bit more." I answered.

"Well I got a call from an FBI agent a couple days ago."

"What!!!!! What did he want????"

"I don't know. I will have to call him back next week."

"Aren't you worried?" I asked.

"Why?" she said. "I did nothing."

After that exchange, my mind started racing back and forth.

The next day my favorite hooker came in to have her jewelry cleaned. Into her mouth went her finger. This time she had on a very large diamond ring.

While I was cleaning and checking the diamonds for being secure in the mounting, she was looking around the showroom floor. When I came out, I saw her waiting at the watch case.

"Oh Ms. Kaye," I said, "we just got a few new Cartier watches. You might be interested in seeing them."

She smiled and every security guard just about died on the spot. "No, thank you I have just about every watch in the case." She chuckled.

It seems the doctor was very generous. Besides the things he already purchased for her, we had heard he had gotten her a beautiful condo on East Lake Shore Drive. It was small but very expensive. As it turned out the doctor had passed away and the family was trying to claw it back from her.

It seems she had already met another man.

He fell madly in love with her. Now they were engaged. I thought that ring was about 12-14 carats. It was a beautiful emerald cut diamond. He turned out to be in real estate. When she first started visiting the store, we called her Krystal. Now it is Ms. Kaye. Soon it would be Mrs. Somebody. There is nothing like a whore! They find respectability and poof they are ladies! I'm beginning to sound like the people in the back room I thought. She didn't look too bad for the wear and tear. There I go again.

Stein noticed she was in the salon and gave me the third degree. It seems he knew her fiancé. Everything was hush hush. Oh well, I could have cared less.

I was excited about my upcoming vacation. Nick got busy at work, and we had to leave a few weeks later than planned. My boss kept saying "Why don't you cancel your trip? We really need you here." he said.

Not a chance, I thought. I just smiled and said, "No."

During this delay, I learned a lot about Yori. He had a family but was living with another man. He seemed to be busy redressing the window displays that we had at several upscale hotels surrounding our store. Mr. Stein thought he did an amazing job. I never saw his work, but we got quite a few sales from this. I guess he was good. Judy was a good salesperson as well. She was personable and had a funny sense of humor. She helped Rosa out with new inventory.

He hired another salesperson. Her name was Angelina. She was the same age as Judy. He exclaimed one day that we needed to find younger people. GG and Mary will retire and then I will be in deep trouble. Angelina was Italian. Although she was born in the United States. She had spent a number of years living in Italy with her husband. She was very experienced and a nice lady. She also spoke Italian, and it came in handy at times.

Yvette had changed her hours because her romance was flourishing, and she was happy to tell his lordship she wanted to slow down. Mr. Stein didn't like it much, but he had no choice. He was a wealthy client and when money was involved Stein couldn't object.

Finally vacation time arrived, and I said adieu to C&F. Ten days of not seeing any of the imbeciles in the back room! Yay! I would miss the good people on the sales floor, but a trip was even better.

Episode 40:

Cheerio and Away We Go!

To say it was luxurious was an understatement! It was super deluxe all the way!

Everything was so wonderful. The plane was a dream. The first-class cabin was super elegant. We went on British Air, and I must say, everything was deluxe. The Brits believed in the true upper class! In fact I think they invented it. We had dinner before we left in the first-class lounge.

After the flight took off, we were served champagne and caviar, and another scrumptious meal was served. I could not eat another bite. Then they gave us pajamas! Nick kept his nose in his papers. In fact, I don't think he slept much. About an hour before arriving in London they woke us up. Then they turned the beds back into seats. We were then served omelets, or pancakes. There was fresh fruit, yogurt, hot rolls and all kinds of teas.

Upon arrival, there was a chauffeur that knew Nick and waved to him.

We had a beautiful Bentley and after we were safely tucked in our seats we departed.

The hotel was magnificent! I found a quirk of Nicks. We did have an amazing super suite as he stated. However, he insisted we carry our own suitcases. I thought that was strange. He was extremely polite but insisted we could manage fine. He was never cheap, so this was strange. The suite was amazing. We had two bedrooms, a living room and just off the living room you stepped up 3 stairs, into our own Solarium. It was spring but still chilly. It had a door to go outside but it was not the weather for it. The view was half of London! We had dinner at a favorite place of his and it was superb.

The next ten days went by in a flash!

I was wined and dined. I was shown the best of everything London had to offer. We had high tea at the Connaught Hotel and high tea at the Ritz. It was Harrods and Knightsbridge for shopping.

We went to seven plays just as Nick had promised. We took day trips to Oxford and the Cotswolds. We visited Westminster Abbey and took a tour to Windsor Castle. Actually I was exhausted! Keeping up with Nick wasn't easy. In the afternoon, on three different occasions we sat in the beautiful conservatory atrium and had snacks and cocktails. He was extremely loving and romantic. About the fourth day I decided we should be intimate. He never pushed me in that regard.

He was a total gentleman. He was gentle and sweet. He was a good lover, and I knew I was headed for trouble. All this elegance and everything plus romance. It was London at our feet. I did not want it to end! One day after we had been together, he took me shopping. We looked at clothes and leather accessories. I picked out a few things and he came into the dressing room with me! I guess the salespeople see this all the time because no one said anything!

I was slightly embarrassed, but he was so much fun. Now I know what it feels like when men buy expensive things for women and play around in our offices. I didn't care!

On the night we didn't have a play to attend, we just had a simple dinner in our room. We enjoyed London by night as the twinkling lights lit the sky pink, dusk became evening. The stores were still busy with shoppers and people just rushing about. We could see the Thames, the Ferris wheel and London Bridge. It was crystal clear outside and so very romantic! He had a special meal prepared and we split some wonderful wine. There was a very beautiful fireplace I had never noticed before. I wanted the evening to never end!

He asked me if I had enjoyed my time with him. I wanted to jump up and down screaming, Yes, yes, yes!

I became very reserved and told him, "Not bad Nick. If you were trying to impress me, you succeeded!"

He laughed. "When we go home, do you think you will still have time for me?"

I looked deep into his eyes and told him, "If you keep all this glamor up you will have a difficult time trying to get rid of me!"

"Gia, we have to go back to the real world in two days. We have been on somewhat of a rollercoaster. I've enjoyed myself and I would like to continue seeing you. I had hoped that you would feel the same way."

Episode 41:

Nick, A Man Who Lets You Know What is On His Mind

I had such a great time in London. The thought of returning to Chicago was like ice water in my face!

"I need to be frank with you and tell you something." Nick said. "There is one thing you will learn to know about me. If I'm thinking something it will come out of my mouth. I don't want to offend you. I do not mince words."

Here it comes, I thought. Something is going to be dropped right on my head and turn this magic to shit.

"You live in a dump." he said. "If we are going to continue. I have to get you out of that shithole where you are living." My face fell to the floor. "I'm sorry. I know I'm frank, but I needed to tell you this." he said.

"I'm sorry if my living accommodations are not up to your quality but it's what I can afford."

"Well I would like to move you out of there."

Tears started to run down my face. He started to laugh. He didn't know I was offended.

"I'm not good enough because my apartment is small?"

"No, You are a doll, but I can't visit you in that shit hole. I'm going to move you to a better place."

"Nick, I can't afford better right now."

"You can't, but I can!"

"Listen, if you want to buy me something nice," I said, "buy me a watch."

"You don't need a watch." he said. "I only will buy you what you need. You need a better place to live. I remember you telling me your girlfriend is a real estate agent."

"Yes?" I answered still confused.

"Call her up now and tell her I want to find a condo that's definitely more appealing. Listen Gia, I think you are confused. I will upgrade your condo. I will pay for it, and it will be better for both of us. Call her now and let me talk to her."

I took his phone, called Barbi, and told her I was calling her from London. "No kidding." she said. "What's going on?"

"I'm going to let you speak to my friend Nick. He asked to speak with you regarding real estate." I handed his phone back to him.

"Hi, I know you are Gia's friend. I want you to line up some condos that are larger than where she is living at the present time. We will be home in two days. Do me a favor and get looking."

"What's your budget?"

"I don't know yet. Just show us some properties that are nice."

"When we find the right place, I will let you know. Here's Gia." and he handed his phone back to me.

"Is he for real?" she asked me.

"I think so." I replied.

That was it. The next day we visited a gallery, and he saw some paintings he liked. "Do you like them?" he asked.

"Yes, they are gorgeous."

He thought about it for a moment and said, "I think I better get you the place first and gingerbread last."

The next day we flew home. I still did not believe what he had said. I told my son, and he just said wow!

Everyone at work was anxious to hear about my trip but I wasn't sharing too much. Don't misunderstand, I was close to most of the salespeople. I just wanted to keep most of what went on private and special. Even Barbi gave me the third degree. I didn't want to share my private time with Nick with anyone.

Three days later Barbi asked me if I wanted to go looking for condos?

"I will call Nick and see when he is free."

"Do you want to look first?" she asked.

"No, I have no idea what he wants to spend."

In between this crazy time, I was busy trying to make a living. My mind constantly drifted away all the time and I had to keep yanking myself back to reality.

Mr. 60's Rock Band Beverly Hills came back and asked for me. I spent a good hour trying to find a certain watch he wanted. Unfortunately, it was out of stock. I lost a sale. At this time, I didn't care.

He said, "Gia, I'm sorry I wanted to purchase it from you but maybe next time."

Mr. Stein gave me the third degree. I didn't care! Also, Ms. Charity Lady, who was a snooty East Lake Shore Drive snob, came into the store. She was the one who pretended to be my friend, and her girlfriend had been married to Yvette's boyfriend.

"I came in looking for you last week. I needed something."

"I was in London on vacation," I answered.

"Really, a tour?" she inquired.

"No, a private vacation with a friend."

"OHHHH!" Was her response. I just smiled.

Some people think they are better than everyone else. That is usual at Cooper and Flux.

Episode 42:

Something is Missing

I received a call from Rosa to please come up to the second-floor loft.

I went upstairs to see Rosa, Jax and Joe Brickmann. "Hi guys, what can I help you with?"

Rosa had a strange look on her face.

Joe said, "Hey Gia, nothing special but did you sell a Cartier Stainless steel bracelet watch and forgot to write it up?"

"Are you kidding? I felt the wrath of Bernard Stein before." I answered. "When I was in London, I didn't sell anything."

"Ok, just checking." he said.

"Ok Joe, what's up?" I asked.

"The old man doesn't know but we are missing a few watches. I thought I would check the sales staff before I reported it. I don't want to alarm anyone if it's nothing. I especially don't want to get the salespeople in trouble.

Joe said, "He better report it to the old man, so there would be no problem. He would certainly ask him why he hadn't said anything before."

"How many?" I asked.

"It looks like two for now."

"Check the usual suspects." I said. "Maybe someone has a couple on hold. Julie is notorious for putting things on hold without writing anything down."

Joe said to say nothing further.

The next day my favorite hooker came in for a jewelry cleaning. She asked for me and said "I just wanted to let you know when I needed a repair or a cleaning I will send in my butler. His name is Trevor, and he will ask for you." Not waiting for a response, she turned on her heels and was out the door in three seconds.

I had a few sales the next day. At least I knew I was productive.

Episode 43:

Shopping

Barbi called me and said she had a few places to show us, whenever we were available.

I called Nick and he said make it tomorrow. I have some appointments today. I really didn't expect him to follow through. Men say a lot of things in the heat of intimacy.

Nick didn't do that. When he said something, he meant it!

We met Barbi at 11:00 am and she showed us a number of nice places. I told her the ones she showed me were nice but pricey. Also, I wasn't fond of Lake Shore Drive because in the winter it got really cold with the blowing wind off the lake.

I really like Streeterville. You are protected by buildings. In fact, I said I like a certain apartment build-ing. It is on East Chestnut, and it is beautiful. She looked in her multiple listings and found a studio, a one-bedroom and two two-bedrooms. I pulled her on the side. I have no idea how much he wants to spend so show him the studio. I would be thrilled to live in that. I told Nick we have a start. We went up to the studio which faced due west. It had a gorgeous view of the city. It was about the same size as my one bedroom but there was a bright light and a view.

He stepped inside and without walking around he said, "NO!"

"Too expensive?" she asked.

"No, it's too small!"

"Should I tell you how much it costs first before you decide?"

"No," he said annoyed. "I want a bigger place."

She took us up to a one bedroom which faced due east and had a lake view. He stepped in and took ten steps inside. It was almost double the size of my apartment.

"No." he said and gestured his thumb down.

"Nick, what do you mean?" she asked.

"It's too small, dear."

"The cost is $376,000."

"I didn't ask you how much did I?"

"Nick, it's really nice." I said.

"No." he said emphatically.

She took her book out and found three other apartments. The first was a small two bedroom. "I feel cramped, he said." The price was $525,000.

The next one was a corner unit. It had an east view, west view and North view.

"Wow!" I said.

"Gia, I have a question for you. If I buy a unit here for you and you need to pay the assessment and taxes, can you afford them?"

The assessment was $800 a month, taxes were about $5,500 a year. "Yes." I said.

"I don't know if we'll be together forever, and I don't want to leave you hanging by not being able to pay for the taxes. Do you like it?"

"It's great." I said.

Look around again and let's see something else to make a comparison.

"Listen Nick, you don't have to do this." I said. Barbi threw me a shut-up look. "I would really like a watch." I said.

"Listen honey, I don't like jewelry, and you don't need a watch. You need a decent apartment."

I looked around as Nick got a call and he excused himself. Barbi and I went to really examine the place. What's this, I stopped. Right in the hallway of the master bedroom was a huge jacuzzi tub.

"I don't like this, Barbi!" I exclaimed.

"Fussy aren't we."

"Listen if I am to live here it should be what I want."

Nick rejoined us and said, "What the hell is this? Forget this place. Gia, do you like it?"

"No, the jacuzzi is in the wrong place and I won't use it."

"Ok Barbi, on to something else or call us when something else comes up on the market." he said.

She went back to her book and said that another unit had just come on the market. Let's see if it can be shown. She made a call, and we went up to the 21st floor. It had the same east, north and west views. The living room had some kind of ugly carpet. The kitchen was open to the living room with a breakfast bar. The entry and kitchen were the most beautiful shade of light apricot marble. The master bedroom had a white carpet that was slightly soiled. The master bath was travertine marble with a Kohler small jacuzzi. The second bedroom was so nice. It had a beige sort of carpet.

"I don't like the carpet in the living room." I said.

"What would you like?" Nick asked.

"I would love hardwood."

"Okay, that's no big deal," he replied, "we can change it. The carpet in the master has to be changed too."

He checked the bedroom and the bath in the guest room. I like the shower because it's a nice size and has marble flooring. The bedroom is good enough too.

"What about parking?" he asked.

"It's not included," she answered back. "There is a garage space but its extra."

"Okay, what are they asking?"

"$730,000. I almost passed out. Plus the garage for $45,000."

"Tell them, I am offering $680,000 cash including the garage."

"Cash?" she said.

"Cash." he replied.

"In your name then?"

"NO! I want it in her name."

"Do you want to be on it as a co purchaser?"

"Listen Barbi, I write the check, and it is in her name only. I want the garage included. Write it up, and I will give you a check for a fifteen thousand dollar deposit, or do you want more?"

"That's fine," she said, "I will present your offer."

He turned to me. "I think it's good enough," he said. "Are you sure you like it, and you can afford the slightly higher assessment and taxes?"

"Yes," I said. I had a hard time catching my breath.

"Let's go. I don't want you to be late for work." He drove me back and dropped me off at the store.

The security guards saw the Ferrari and almost broke their legs running to the door to see it. As it happened, Julie saw it too. She was coming back from lunch.

She walked straight to the back room and didn't even say a word to me. "Nichols hit pay dirt over here. Where did she meet him? Is he your customer Bern?"

Mr. Stein had been distracted and answered "What?"

"Gia Nichols over here has a wealthy boyfriend. Did you know that?"

"No, I didn't," he said. "Who is he Nichols? Did you meet him here?"

"No, I did not. It is no one's business who I date! For everyone's information, he was the man you wanted to throw out because he wasn't dressed good enough for you. He bought his daughter that diamond necklace. Julie was very pissed!"

"What was it to her?"

"She went to London with him." Mary said.

"How and where did she meet him?" Stein and Julie said in unison.

Mary replied, "Ask her, I don't know."

I had walked out before the exchange but was upset that they needed to know my business! All I know Mary said is that he's her boyfriend.

Episode 44:

My Business and Only My Business

That night I went to dinner at The Place with Barbi. She told me the FBI agent called her again and made an appointment to see her at the Daley Center.

"Aren't you worried?" I asked.

"Hell no! I didn't do anything wrong Gia."

Just then, in walks Mr. Stein with Skippy Houseman and their wives. They stopped at our table and Mr. Stein talked to Barbi and asked her how she was enjoying her jewelry? He then turned to me.

"You two girls are all alone, eh?"

"Looks like it." she answered back sharply.

He smiled and they walked by and went to their table. Toni came over about thirty minutes later and stopped by our table. "You both seem to be the hot topic over at the Houseman and Stein Table."

Barbi turned to Toni and said, "Fuck 'em!"

Jealousy comes in every price point and all colors of green.

A few minutes later, Barbi met an old friend, and they were going across the street to Jilly's for a drink.

They invited me but I was going home.

Nick called me and asked if I heard anything.

"No." I answered. "Everyone was asking about your car at work," I said.

"Next time I will drive my Roller. Maybe I'll get Bruce to drive me. Ha, Ha. That would be a hoot, Gia!"

"Nick, there is so much jealousy there. I really would rather you did not."

"Okay, I'll come in and sit on the floor and wait till the security guard throws me out!"

He thought it was so funny. I guess when you are really rich you can be as eccentric as you want to be. Poor people are nuts. Rich people are eccentric.

The next day Barbi called and said, "Congratulations, you might have a new apartment. They accepted your offer. I mean Nick's offer."

I hung up and called him from the phone in the lunchroom.

Vasha, the bitch heard part of my conversation. "Darling, honey, what did I hear? Are you buying a new apartment? I didn't know Mr. Stein paid you so well?"

I didn't look at her. I turned and walked away. I got a page from the floor a client was asking for me.

It was a May/December couple I had worked with in GG's absence. She had been out with the flu.

He was a really nice man. They had been married for about ten years. I think at one time, she was a dancer of some sort. Now she was a society lady. We had a lot of customers like them. I had waited on them a few times. Clients tend to be very loyal. They only wanted me, and they waited while I finished another sale.

He explained to me he wanted to buy her an exceptional ring. I didn't quite understand because she had already an expensive ring. He reminded me that I had a conversation with his wife about the best diamonds.

"Oh yes, I remember. It was a while ago."

"I want to purchase something special for her that she could sell down the road if she ever needs extra money and I am not around."

"Oh yes," I replied, "I was talking to her about Golconda diamonds. They are the best diamonds and are extremely rare."

Only one to two percent of earth grown diamonds are type IIa classified Golconda diamonds. Historically speaking, Golconda diamonds are graded as type IIa. They initially were discovered in the Golconda region in India. They can now be found in other parts of the world. What makes them so special? They are so pure from lack of oxygen during formation of the rough. Golconda diamonds have no measurable nitrogen and lack chemical impurities. The clarity is extremely high. They have been reported as the cleanest, most transparent and intensely brilliant diamonds on Earth. Looking at a Golconda IIa diamond is like looking through pure icy water. These diamonds have been known as diamonds of the finest quality. A few notably famous Golconda gems are the Koh-I Noor, Idol's Eye, and Harry Winston's spectacular Hope Diamond, though that one is a IIb type.

The client wanted a stone between 12 and 15 carats. He of course wanted it to come with papers describing the provenance of the diamond and all specific details related to the stone.

I went to Stein and told him what they were looking for and he said tell them to give me a week.

Bernard Stein said to me, "Okay I will get stones in for you and if you need help call Julie or me in to assist you."

"I don't need assistance," I said. "They are looking for Golconda. A type IIa diamond."

"I know Nichols."

I was walking down Oak Street a couple days later, and there was a big sign. Coming soon diamonds are a girl's Best Friend! I saw one of the finest diamond houses being advertised and I thought to myself. I'm plenty good enough to work there! I know I am!

I made a mental note to make an application to try and get a job there.

I've had enough of the bull shit from Cooper and Flux. I've had enough of Bernard Stein and his band of merry nut cases. I'm not going to say anything to anyone and will wait to see what happens.

About a week later, the boss told me he received three stones in for my customers. One was a Golconda type IIa stone. It was absolutely gorgeous! Perfect for them. The other two were nice stones but that's it.

"Listen Nichols, I want you to sell one of the two stones that are not Golconda. The Golconda is amazing, but I can make more on the other two. I have to pay a lot for the Golconda stone. It has a high premium! Sell the other ones."

I looked at him and said, "NO! I told her about the India Mine. I told her how rare and special the Golconda Type 11a diamonds are. Why should I lie?"

He looked at me and slowly got red in the face. He had a book in his hand and slammed it on the desk. "You do what I tell you to do! Sell the other stones." He started to foam at the mouth. "I don't care which one you sell but not the Golconda one!"

I looked at him and stared at him. I turned on my heels and walked out. I will take the sale from you and sell it myself. "Go ahead," I said back. "I'm not going back on my word."

"You will sell yourself right out of a job! Do you HEAR ME!"

"Wait on them yourself." I said.

The next night Nick and I went to dinner at Tucanos. The food was great, and I tried to be as upbeat as I could. He knew something was wrong. I finally told him. He told me I had two choices. I know, I said.

"Anyway, are you excited about your new apartment?"

"I'm so excited. I could jump up and down right here!" I answered.

He smiled and said to me, "I'm paying for the apartment and the garage. Understand, if we break up, the apartment is still yours. If you decide you want the garage space, you will have to pay for it. No paying back for the apartment, just the garage."

I thought that was odd, but I didn't care. I nodded my head. We had a great time that night. Just like I said before, poor people are crazy. Rich people are eccentric. The next day Barbi gave Nick a closing date. I met with his lawyer and was told he would be with me at the closing. He had a check for the apartment. That was about it.

I had never heard of paying cash for an apartment.

The closing date was set for two weeks. I couldn't believe it. Barbi called Nick and again asked if he wanted it in his name. He lost his temper and asked her, "How many times must I tell you?"

"Okay," she tried to soothe him, "we will do as you wish."

"Don't worry. My lawyer will be with her."

"End of story!" he said.

Episode 45:

The Golconda Diamond and Other Matters

The next day my clients came in. Stein walked in and told them I was busy with another customer and couldn't wait on them. The wife stood up and said, "We are leaving. I want only Gia."

"You have the owner here. I've forgotten more than she will ever know." Stein insultingly said about me.

She stuck to her guns. "It's Gia or it's no one."

He started with her and told her he would advise her to take one of the other two diamonds. They were as good without the hefty price tag.

Her husband replied, "Honey it's up to you."

"Gia or no one." she replied.

Stein got up and told them to wait until Gia was finished.

He walked in back to where I was sitting and told me to wait five minutes and go to them. He was as mad as I've ever seen him. I wouldn't endanger my integrity for him to make more money on this!

Yes, I always do as I'm told but I will not lie to a client, not ever.

I went in and talked about all three diamonds. I told her the pros and cons of all the stones. I told her if she decided on the Golconda, she would be paying more because it has a book on its provenance.

She looked at all three and bluntly asked me, "What would you do?"

I said, "If it's about money go with one of the others. If you want a stone that will always be worth more on the market, it's the Golconda type 11a and only that one."

She said to her husband, "Honey, I want the Golconda. That's what I would do sweetheart."

One million dollars and it was sold! I had the highest one item sale. Others have sold multiple items for more money, but my sale was special!

She was so happy. She said, "I knew you would be honest with me!"

Here I go, I thought, right on the street!

Stein looked at me that night and said, "Good sale, Gia."

"Thank you, Mr. Stein." I answered.

Joe gave me a wink and said, "Good for you Gia. I have something to tell you."

"What? Start looking for a new job, I said? Have you heard something?"

"No, I'm leaving here. I found another job! More money, less hours, and no bull shit, I hope."

I was stunned. My eyes welled up with tears. "Joe, how will I survive here without you?"

"You will do just fine! I'm not leaving for a couple of months. So don't worry. The store is being built so who knows how long it will be."

I thought it was the famous diamond place down the street. No, it was not.

Joe's upcoming departure from the hell hole hit me like a ton of bricks. He kept reassuring me it would take months. All I could think of was that the one person I could rely on was leaving.

Episode 46:

Welcome Home

The closing day was upon me. I didn't know what to expect. Nick reassured me. All would go well. His lawyer was like white toast. He said it was a pleasure meeting me. He gave the title company the information. He was right, it was only in my name.

He handed over that huge check and I received the keys.

I could not believe what had just transpired. That beautiful sunny apartment with incredible views was mine.

Now I started to worry, yet again. What if the old man fires me. What if, what if, what if. Barbi told me to forget my problems and live in the moment.

I set up a moving day and Nick kept his promise and put in a wooden floor in the living room. I went to see the apartment again and my mouth fell open. It was more beautiful than I remembered. The doormen were even elegant. Everyone was so nice. I had a real washer and dryer! I was happy and worried at the same time. I had not seen the sun in an apartment for over twelve years.

On moving day, I was beside myself. My little cat had not seen the sun her entire life with me. She hid for three days! My old apartment had another apartment right in front of mine. There was just a view of another apartment. It was about two hundred feet from my windows. You could look down and see trees and people walking but that was it. When I closed the door on the old apartment, I felt like a new person.

I cannot tell you how difficult it was to sleep the first night in my new condo. So many things kept running through my mind. I chanted for happiness in front of my shrine.

The next day, I had to tell the old Vasha at work to change everything to my new address.

"Oh Gia, I know you do not receive commission. How is this possible?"

I looked at her and said, "I don't think it's your business, is it?" She backed off. There was plenty of talk in the back room. Joe and his wife knew but they were the only people I told.

Nick and I continued to do well in our relationship. We had many wonderful dinners together. We went to many charity events together. People in the back office finally figured I was one of the lucky girls who had a boyfriend who bought them an apartment.

Nick bought me a new television for my bedroom. "My girlfriend, Gina, had a television she didn't use. She brought it downtown and we put it in my new den."

I had my carpet in the master bedroom cleaned and it looked pretty good.

I was so happy.

Nick did not care for the long commute into the city. I heard about it often enough.

He had an issue with one of his companies, so he gave the cruise away to an employee. He said he would make it up to me. Frankly, I didn't care.

After getting my beautiful condo, I felt like I was in paradise daily. That was until I had to go to work.

In the late summer he took me to the Bahamas, and we flew in a private jet. It was amazing.

We had great meals, of course, and we stayed at The Ocean Club. The water was crystal blue. We had amazing weather. I bought a new bikini and if I do say so myself, I looked pretty good in it.

Nick made a comment that I took his breath away. That's all I needed to hear. However, we did have an issue. He loved to ride motorcycles, and I did not. He was in his mid-70's and his reflexes were not that great. Riding on the back of a motorcycle was not my idea of fun. One time we were riding along in the Bahamas. He misjudged a turn, and we wiped out. I got a burn from the pavement and fell on my ankle. He thought it was funny that he wiped out.

I did not!

Back in Chicago I thought about our relationship. He was a great guy. He had his troubling moments. He drove his Ferrari way too fast. He drove the motorcycle fast and his reflexes were slow. I did not want to get injured because he had a death wish!

I told him he was a great guy but lived too much on the edge. I suggested we take a break for a while.

He was disappointed but not to where he was going to do things differently.

I said nothing to anyone except Barbi.

She wanted me to rethink this relationship, but I was adamant.

She advised me to get back on the dating site. However, I was not in any hurry.

Episode 47:

Thieves and Other Creeps

Joe thankfully had not changed his job because the building took a long time, and he was upset with the whole process.

We were in limbo in life and in work. Except, something strange was going on.

Business was brisk.

We were all busy and time passed.

Barbi heard back from the FBI. It took a long time.

Finally, this agent called her and asked her to come down to the Daley Center for questioning.

I didn't hear from her for hours. I kept asking myself, what was going on?

Finally, she called and left a message with Rosa. She wanted me to stop by her house after work.

It was a busy day, and I was wiped out. I needed to hear what was happening.

I crossed the street hoping all would be okay. I thought about why I was wiped out. It wasn't only because I was so busy. I needed to give answers to the head man and his cronies. Everyone was accountable for their entire day. 'Why didn't they make a sale? Why did the customer leave without getting information on the item? Why didn't they make another appointment? Why? Why?' I was mentally exhausted. Stein was a big part of the problem. Sometimes he would ask why someone was off the floor for so long? All that time!? I felt like I had to report everything all the time.

That same day there was a cruel incident between the sales associate GG and Mr. Stein. GG was getting on in age and sometimes she would nod off. When we talk about down time that could be several hours. Mary also nodded off occasionally. As a matter of fact, if you wait for hours and no one comes into the salon it is easy for anyone to fall asleep! Unfortunately, Stein was watching the monitor one day.

He got up and went over to GG's desk and shouted, "GG, the salon is on fire, save yourself!" She did not move! He yelled again and this time she woke up.

She looked at him and asked, "Did you say something?"

He laughed at her, but he was angry. We told her what happened and the next day she went to an audiologist and found out she had a wax build up in her ears and was slightly deaf. Stein had no compassion for her. Believe me when I tell you, the lady was an excellent sales lady and could outsell the best of them. I felt sad for her as did Mary.

That day was an especially long one for me, so I took my coat and walked across the street to Barbis' condo. She had a glass of wine waiting for me.

"Sit down." she said. She proceeded to tell me about her day with the FBI. "The agents wanted to know how well I knew that guy that looked like Bill Clinton. They took my phone and looked him up. They found I was telling the truth. I didn't really know him. We had a couple of dinners, but I noticed there was something off about him. I never mentioned when he took his clothes off and chased me around my apartment. Some things are just too personal. They found my number on his phone along with a lot of other women. They told me I was a lucky one. The agents suspected he had murdered his wife, but a body was never found. They found blood and tissue but no body. He also threatened a few ladies he had been seeing. He told all the ladies he had been seeing that he was a single man. Eventually, they found a suspected murder weapon. He was in jail. His alibi did not match from what he had told them in the beginning. The neighbors added a lot to the story. There were a lot of arguments and eventually his wife disappeared. The agents told me I was lucky. I hope he rots in that place. That poor woman. Who knows where she is."

Barbi asked if I wanted to go to dinner. I had enough. Between work and her story, I was exhausted.

Episode 48:

Thieves

The next couple of weeks flew by. I went on a couple of dates but nothing special. Joe called me up to the loft.

"Listen Gia, we have another situation."

"What?" I asked.

"Rosa is missing 12 Cartier watches. Please go through your sales. Do you have anything on hold?"

"No." I answered.

"Okay don't discuss this. Stein is, of course, upset. Say nothing, we want to keep this quiet. It's an internal problem. I'm only asking the people I trust."

"How long has this been happening?" I asked.

"Rosa thinks about a year."

"You know what?" I asked. "Remember the Henry Dunay watch I used to wear?"

"Sure, why?"

"Well a couple of months ago I asked Yori about it. I like to wear it occasionally and I hadn't seen it in a while. He said it is on display at one of the hotels. I said, 'No it's not! I was just there on a date, and it was not in any window.' Mr. Peepers overheard our conversation and stated, 'Nichols, you are living high on the hog, aren't you?' and Yori said, 'Okay it is probably in repair for some issue.' 'Okay.' I answered. That was it. Nothing was ever mentioned again, and I forgot about it.

"Rosa," Joe said, "see if you can track down the Dunay watch."

A couple weeks before this incident, I saw a sign go up on the Diamonds are Forever store. I decided to send them my resumé. I did not hear anything, so I did not mention it to anyone.

Around that time, I met an interesting man on the dating site. At first, I was hesitant. He lived out of state. I didn't think it would become anything. He was about twelve years older than me and was a widower.

His name was Gregory. He was very nice. He was tall and very smart. He owned his own company. He did a lot of business in Chicago and all over the globe. I thought he was charming. I was always attracted to smart, interesting men. He was a take charge type of guy. He never went to college, but you wouldn't know it. He told me he learned a lot from being an officer in the Army. He patterned his life after some friend of his family's that was very successful. He always wanted to own his own company, after he finished his time in the army. He started selling heavy machinery. When he got the opportunity, he went out on his own. Although he started with nothing, now he was quite well off. As usual, men always tried to impress you with how accomplished they were. He was not a bullshit kind of guy, or so I thought. I enjoyed being with him. He was charming, although not prince charming. He was nice looking. He did not remind me of Nick. Nick wasn't Prince Charming either.

Does a perfect guy even exist?

He would come into Chicago every two weeks, and we would go to dinner. He liked to dance and was a pretty good dancer. We would go to the Drake hotel. They had a Jazz band that was amazing. We always had fun.

There was one drawback. I had adopted a little dog. I also had my cat Zoey. He wasn't an animal person. I did not like that. If you like me, accept my animals or hit the road, Jack. He wasn't rude or abusive to them. He just didn't like petting them. I thought wait and see. I was glad I had my beautiful apartment.

Our relationship heated up. We had a great summer and fall seemed promising. He was as all the other men I had met. He had this. He's been here. He's done this. He told me all about his past girlfriends. He especially went on about the last one who was a European. She was a gold digger or so he said. I never asked him about any of them because I didn't care. He showed me her picture. She was nothing. She looked like something that the cat dragged in and should have left outside. I do not like gold diggers. If the man or woman was married that as we know is a big NO, NO for me. Anyone that goes after a married person will have the same thing done to them. I always remembered my experience with Pat. Gregory was not married when he dated the European. I was also wary about men who talked about past girlfriends. He told me the first lady he dated after his wife passed away was crazy. This second one was a gold digger. It takes two, doesn't it?

Our relationship was pretty hot for an older man.

Episode 49:

Intrigue

Meanwhile at work, nothing was really happening. Joe was getting ready to make his move. I was unhappy about that. The missing watches were still missing. The beautiful Henry Dunay watch was gone as well. It had disappeared into thin air.

Mr. Peepers and I were not getting along either. He was trying to stick his nose into my sales. He said he wanted to help me. Listen, I neither asked for his help nor needed it. Things were not going well.

One day a very pretty young woman came into the salon. It was Judy's turn, but she asked me to help her out and take this one. I said sure. The customer came in and waited for someone to approach her. She was about twenty-five years old. She had long black hair. She was dressed professionally. She was sexy, in a very aristocratic way. She told me she came from Persia to the United States when she was a young child. She said her name was Azar and that her work was in advertising. She wanted to find a birthday gift for her sister. She hoped to find something special. She asked me about a peridot ring. Her sister loved green. She could not afford an emerald. That was my first thought.

I wanted to send her over to the French salon. I had worked there, and they had exactly what she was asking about. Of course I would never do that.

At the time I worked at that salon, I sold a lovely crossover ring. One side was a peridot, and the other side was an amethyst. It would be perfect for her. I knew it was exactly what she was looking for.

However, my job was to show the customer what we had. I did my best to show her a lot of pretty things. Nothing similar to a peridot ring. She laughed and told me she knew I didn't have what she was looking for. However, she recognized I was taking my time with her. She said she believed I had shown her half of our inventory.

"You know I knew you did not have a peridot ring. However, you are taking your time and engaging in your attitude.

Mr. Peepers came out of nowhere and introduced himself. I threw him a dirty look. I wanted to say what the hell do you want?

"Sometimes two pairs of eyes are better than one." he stated. "Maybe I can offer some assistance to you both."

"Sure." I replied.

I really wanted to call him a little twerp and tell him to get lost.

I said nothing. She told him, "You are so kind, but Gia was really taking her time with me and although she appreciated his offer, we were fine."

Bravo, I thought!

He slimed his way out of there.

We continued on. Finally, as she gave me her name, she told me, "Gia, you have given me plenty to think about. Perhaps, I may have found something I'm interested in. Could you please give me your card and I will consider my options and get back with you."

"Absolutely." I said. "I will ask for your name and number and perhaps if I find something wonderful, I will give you a call."

"Sure." she said. Azar gave me her number. As she left, she saw Mr. Peepers and waved to him.

I thought there was a classy young lady. I enjoyed working with her.

I walked in the back and Stein was waiting for me. "You took your sweet time with that one Nichols. What happened?"

"We didn't have what she wanted. I tried to sell her something else, but she wasn't interested."

Out of nowhere the Twerp showed himself. "I tried to help her, Mr. Stein, but she didn't want any assistance."

"Why not Nichols?"

"The client didn't appreciate the intrusion, sir. I got her information and if something comes in, I will call her. In fact, I will give her a week and call her anyway just to touch base."

He shook his head and said, "Write it in the book, whatever you showed her."

He didn't have to tell me this. I knew the drill.

Episode 50:

My Romantic Life and More Intrigue

I got a call from Gregory, and he said he was coming into Chicago on the weekend. Would I be available?

We had a very romantic weekend. He was a very robust lover. He asked me if I would like to visit his home. He wanted to show me his house and his business. He was adding on to his building and needed to get approval from the city council in the area. Would I be interested? I told him sure. He bought me a ticket and though Mr. Stein bitched about it all, I went.

While I was gone, someone tried to lift a piece of jewelry from the ring case. He didn't get anywhere and was taken into custody.

Once I was joking with the guards, about what ifs? Scott, one of the security guards, said, "Gia, if there is an incident and we go to guns, remember to duck! We might have to sacrifice a hostage for the sake of everyone else. I would hate for it to be you. Remember to duck or hit the floor." Were they being funny or real? I never knew.

Anyway, I was in Gregory's home state and was having a great time. His family was very nice. We had wonderful dinners. All in all, I enjoyed myself. I really started to have feelings for him. This concerned me. I didn't want to get hurt. Typical response for me. Who wants to get hurt? I returned back to Chicago.

The day I returned to work Joe was cleaning out his desk. 'You will do fine Gia. Always CYA—Cover your Ass. Remember, I'm right next door. He was too. It was literally next door. "What about the boss I asked. I know for a fact she's a real bitch.'

"I can take care of myself," he replied. "Remember, I worked for Bernard Stein. I also worked for his father. That gives you the experience to handle whatever is thrown at you. How will Rosa and Jax do without you?"

"They will be fine. Jax has his porn and Rosa is always busy."

"Now Gia, remember if it comes to lie detector tests, you take it. Also, tell the Big Caboose. I will take one as well. He knows where to find me."

A few more sobs, goodbyes and good luck.

The minute he left I knew Bernard Stein felt pressure. Joe did everything. There was no one like him and he knew he was up shits creek without him.

Julie, his big manager, was as useless as could be. Daniel, (Mr. Peepers) said he could take over for Joe. That was a bigger joke than Julie. Nothing was worse than Julie taking his spot. She was a complete con concerning everything. She loved to play the blame game. She always tried to put the problem and blame on someone else. As she got older, her memory got worse. She drank more, although never at work. Sometimes you could smell it on her in the morning. She also put on weight. If something was wrong, she would question one of us forever. I was waiting for the missing Cartier watches. Nothing was ever said.

Gregory and I had made a plan to get together for my birthday which was December 15th. His was the 20th of December. We were going to celebrate together.

I got a call from him telling me he had caught the flu and would not be coming as we had discussed. He thought he would be better in a few days. After a week, I became worried. I tried calling him. He did not answer. I texted and did not get a response. Finally, I was going to call his son because Gregory was in his 70's and you never know. I thought I would get a plane ticket and surprise him. He needed me. He was always good about calling. Before I bought the ticket, I called his son Chad. I told him my concerns and he assured me his dad was fine, just very busy. He told me he would have his dad contact me and not to worry. I didn't think I would be so affected. I was so worried. The next day I got a text.

My ex-girlfriend came to take care of me while I was sick. We decided to try and get back together.

THAT WAS IT. No goodbye, no good luck, no fuck you. All I got was a text! It was now a few days before my birthday. I can't tell you how stunned I was. I called in sick and stayed in bed for three days! I couldn't believe how he had touched me. I should have just forgotten him. I curled up in the fetal position and did nothing else.

Finally, I said to the walls, "Gregory, eat shit and die!"

My son knew how hurt I was. He was the only one I told. Barbi also knew but she never knew how much I cared about him. I always tried to keep my feelings private. He was a low life sneaking liar. I was better off without him. I told my broken heart this every day.

Episode 51:

A Surprise Gift!

I got a call from Azar after returning to work. She was the lady that wanted the peridot ring. She asked me if we could meet for coffee. I thought that was strange. Sure, I said, and made a date for the next week. I told no one.

It was my turn for a new client. A man who could have been a vagrant walked in. Mr. Peepers told me "It's your up Nichols. Good luck!"

I walked out and saw a man who looked like he needed a meal, not jewelry. He had a baseball cap pulled down around his head and a soiled light weight jacket. It was cold and he needed a heavier coat. He said he was looking for an engagement ring. We talked for quite a while. I got some pictures out and he pointed to a ring. He was extremely specific.

He asked, "How long it takes to get that kind of quality into the store?"

I answered, "I could have it in the salon in a few days." He took my card and gave me his information and off he went.

I got a feeling about him. The guard at my desk told me he heard the entire exchange. Did I want him thrown out if he returned? I said if you do, we will lose a big sale. He called me and we made a date to meet again. I was told all kinds of crap from the other sales associates.

"Gia, that one is a loser." Mary said. "I will have him thrown out if he returns."

"NO!" I said emphatically. "I got the diamonds in for him. I went over Mr. Stein's head and went to Rosa."

"This will be expensive Gia."

"I know," I replied. "Please just get them in for me."

"Sure she said, no problem."

The next time I saw him he was wearing the exact same outfit, only a little more soiled. I took him into a diamond room and after about one hour.

He said he would let me know tomorrow. "I want my fiancé to come and see the ring as well."

I gave him the price of $250,000. He did not flinch. I went into the back and Mr. Stein flew into a rage. "You went over my head Gia. Who do you think you are? YOU did not tell me anything about him and you ordered some very expensive diamonds. What gives you the right?" Julie rolled her eyes and snickered.

I left the back room, and the guard intervened. "Gia, what are you doing?"

"Listen Ralph, I know this man is for real."

"You're the boss." he said. "I need to be standing outside the room when and if he visits next."

"Sure." I said.

The boss came out and dragged me into a room. "You are overstepping, Gia Nichols. Joe is not here to save you. If this does not sell, I'm docking you the cost of ordering these very expensive diamonds in without my approval. Got that?"

"Yes sir." I answered.

"You're a good salesperson but you do not own the store, and I have to be aware of everything."

"Do you want me to turn over the sale to someone else?" I asked.

"Hell NO!" he shot back. "He will not buy, and no one wants this mess on their record."

I mentioned a favorite salesperson of his and he said NO as loud as could be. I remembered an incident with this one. We always had to ask for special days off if there was a doctor's appointment. My name was on the calendar for a mammogram for weeks. At the last minute she had said to the boss, she needed the day as well. He was already angry with me, so he told me to cancel my appointment. I had told him no emphatically. I don't want to get cancer. He was angry with me about the diamonds, so this was his last straw. His special salesperson wanted a day off and I would not change my appointment to accommodate her.

He turned and said to me, "I hope you get cancer! You do not deserve the day!" I went into the ladies room and cried.

That afternoon, a lady asked for me and waited while I finished up with another client. She was the fiancé of Mr. Vagrant. She was dressed quite well and told me she was a lawyer with a firm I was familiar with.

Instead of me telling the back room the story, I kept quiet. She loved the diamonds and the setting. She also said her fiancé was very impressed with me for the way I did business. She explained he was a professional gambler and was extremely superstitious. A light went on in my head. I remembered there was a show every Saturday from Las Vegas. My son would watch it, and he told me the guys that gamble professionally would dress like they needed a meal ticket. They didn't want to ruin their good luck. I said nothing to anyone.

Mr. Vagrant came in just as he said he would. Again, he was wearing the exact same clothes. The guard waited outside the door. I had to explain it was common practice for such fine goods. He was not concerned. He told me his fiancé liked me and loved the diamonds. He pulled out a check book and a Black American Express Card. He wrote a check and gave me his credit card to hold the diamonds.

He thanked me for dealing with his quirks and I said, "I do not know what you mean? You are a delight to work with and so is your fiancé."

He said, "You are too kind, but I will be purchasing any and all gifts from you in the future."

I walked quietly in the back. Everyone was waiting. Julie cracked a low-class joke as only she could.

"Well Nichols," Stein shot at me. "are you ready to write a nice check for the transfer of the diamonds?"

"I have a check here," I said quietly, "and a Black American Express Card."

I didn't know who was going to fall over first. Joe would have been proud of me. Vasha moved her big fat ass and almost lost her wig. Rosa and Jax and Mary were applauding. That is the end of that story. Mr. Vagrant became a regular client of mine.

It was time for me to meet Azar. I didn't understand what she wanted with me. I learned never to ask a client anything.

I met her at the coffee shop Starbucks on Rush Street. She was strikingly beautiful and very engaging.

"I guess you are wondering what this is all about." she said with a slight smile.

"Yes, quite frankly I am a little puzzled."

"Gia, I have a sister, but I was not looking for a peridot ring as I stated. I am looking for great talent. I know I have found the BEST in you."

"I do not understand Azar." I replied.

"I work for the premiere Diamond and Jewelry House in New York and soon to be in Chicago. We are looking for the best of the best."

I must have dropped my mouth to the floor. I sent my resumé to them months ago. If I mention their name, you'd probably know immediately who they are. Marilyn Monroe sang about them in *Diamonds Are A Girl's Best Friend*.

"Your customer service and salesmanship put you at the very top of my list. You are an amazing lady."

I said, "Why thank you. That is so kind."

I'm thinking if Judy only knew who she was turning over to me, she would kick herself. Judy wanted out of C and F as much as I did. I told Azar I had sent in my resumé. I had not heard back. She reassured me. They would rather scout for talent. She offered me an amazing job. She wanted me to help train the other women that would be joining me. She said the commission I would be making alone would put me well over six figures. There would be a generous bonus, IRA'S and salary. I would be most comfortable. I didn't want to sound too excited, but I wanted to kiss her! I asked her if I could think about it for a couple of days.

She handed me her card and said, "Of course dear. Please call me and let me know what you decide. Just ask for me please." After that exchange I wanted to start singing. I thanked her and told her she would be hearing from me.

The next day, I asked my boss for a few minutes of his time. He said, "Nichols you will get an added bonus at the end of the year for your beautiful work with the gambler." He half apologized for his behavior. It wasn't really an apology. I didn't care!

"No, Mr. Stein," I said. "I've been offered a really wonderful sales position with the new store down the street." He looked at me like I had knifed him in the back.

All of a sudden, he was offering me a fifteen thousand dollar raise in salary. He also offered me a fat heavy bonus at the end of the year. "Sorry sir," I said in my nicest voice, "It is too little too late. I will be moving on in a couple of months or possibly sooner. If, however, you want me to leave immediately, I will."

In the jewelry business they sometimes will throw you out the day you give notice. This is done because they are concerned about thefts.

He looked at me as if I had shot him. He put his arm around me and said softly. "Please reconsider. I want you to think about how much you are valued here. After you consider my offer, please let me know what you decide." He started shaking his head. He left the office. I sat there because this was the first time he had ever spoken to me with regard. I could have cared less.

All I could think about was the new salon. No more bull shit abuse for nothing and commission sales!

The word spread quickly in the salon. I was waiting for him to tell me to leave but he didn't. He asked me to stay longer because people will be asking for me. I of course declined.

Somehow, the word got out on the sales floor I was leaving. At the same time, the announcement came that twelve Cartier watches and one Henry Dunay watch were missing. I got a couple of snide remarks directed my way. I said to the people making the comment to line us all up. I'm ready to take a lie detector test or anything else they wanted to direct at me.

Episode 52:

The Memorable Last Day in Hell

My last day at C&F, this happened.

It started out by being like any other Saturday. It was quiet in the morning. After lunch we became busier. Many of the customers were the usual tourists. I never mentioned this before but on Saturdays, we were not to leave the store for anything. Mr. Stein always brought in lunch for the salespeople. The only people that went outside were the smokers. After lunch they would take turns and go outside for a smoke.

An unknown client comes in about 1:30pm asking for a yellow diamond. They wanted a large diamond. I had only one that slightly resembled what they were asking for and it was in the window. Mr. Peepers had been dressing the windows for about a year. He was the only one who had the key. I had to go and ask him for the key. He told me he would go and get the ring out of the window.

"Do you know these people?"

I said to him, "Who do you think you are, Mr. Stein?"

He got the ring and handed it over to me. Then he said, "Keep the key, I'm going upstairs. Rosa needs something."

I took my time showing the 10.00ct yellow diamond. There was something strange about these people. I couldn't put my finger on it. Many times, at other salons, we had people come in and pretend they were shopping. The purpose of this exercise was to see how we behaved and our productivity.

I got this feeling that they were doing just that. I had the same feeling about the lovely Azar at first.

After about forty minutes they said they would think about it and left. I went into the window and replaced the ring. I locked the case and came out. I then had a call for another customer. This couple were Be Backs. Be Backs are people that you have shown items to before and they come into the salon asking for you. I sold them a tennis bracelet for about $6,000.

Stein said "Nice sale, Nichols. Are you sure you want to leave?" I didn't answer but smiled.

It was now closing time, and a big surprise was waiting for me in the lunchroom. It was a beautiful cake with the number ten written on the top. There was a lady drawn on the top of the cake. She was running out the door that was connected to the number ten. Everyone said surprise! Gee it had been ten years at C&F. Time goes by when you're having a good time. Unfortunately,

I was not. I felt sad about my friends but not that sad. We all enjoyed the cake and the small talk. Then it was time to close up the salon. We started pulling the diamond goods out of the display cases and putting them away.

We were almost finished when Mr. Peepers came out of the window display with his tray of goods.

"Nichols, can I have the 10.00ct yellow you pulled out of the window please?"

I looked at him in disbelief. "What are you talking about?" I asked. "I placed it back in the window hours ago."

He then announced that the yellow diamond was not in its place. "Who has it?" No one answered.

Mr. Stein came out of the back and said to the salespeople. "Ok, who was showing the yellow diamond?" I raised my hand. "Where is it?"

"I put it back," I said.

Mr. Peepers looked at me with a smirk. Yori had just returned from the hotel where he had changed the window. No one had to mention it because we would never put a high value item in the hotel display. It was never done. I looked at the two of them and caught a funny expression between them.

"Wait a minute," I said, "I was the only one in the window. Mr. Peepers and I named a few others who had gone outside for smokes. I returned it to the window, and it was there when I locked the display."

"Okay Mr. Stein," I said. "call the police. I want a police woman to strip search me. I'm not leaving the store until I'm exonerated. I want to be examined everywhere."

He looked at me and said, "Nichols, shut up. If anything, YOU ARE NOT A THIEF! Get your things together and leave."

"I wanted a policewoman." I stated. "No one will soil my reputation!"

He yelled at me and told me to leave.

I got my things together through tears streaming down my face. I started here with a stolen story and I'm finishing with a hum dinger.

I walked outside and went to Barbi's. I had forgotten she had a date. I walked home. When I got home, I called Joe Brickmann and told him what happened. He came over with his wife and we all had a good talk. He said he had spoken to Rosa and Jax and something was very peculiar about Mr. Peepers and Yori.

Obviously, I was the patsy. I was completely set up.

He told me to call the store on Monday and demand a lie detector test!

I don't know how I slept that weekend. Monday morning came and at 9:00 am sharp, I called the store.

Mr. Stein was actually very civil. He asked me to come in at 6pm. The guard let me in. Seeing me he said, "You can't stay away, eh?" I went into the store waiting for the staff to leave.

It was dark and very eerie. I walked into the back. There was Mr. Stein and Julie.

He said to me he knew about the twelve Cartier watches and the Henry Dunay watch. He also said, Saturday was an excellent opportunity to frame someone. Since they all knew you were leaving, you were the candidate.

"Gia, I'm sorry, but you have to be questioned. You were a pain in the ass at times here. You are no thief, and we all know it! As far as salespeople go you were one of the best. Please come in. Be questioned like everyone else. You will also be required to take a lie detector test. Are you ok with that?"

"Yes!" I said emphatically.

"Okay, you will be called in a week or two and it shouldn't take too long. Nothing will be said to anyone. I would not jeopardize your new job. Everything will be done quietly."

Two weeks came. Just as Mr. Stein said, I was called to come in for the test and questioning.

Everyone there was as nervous as a whore in church. I chanted the whole weekend. I knew I was innocent. Of course I was nervous. Fear of the unknown. We were put into one room. The girls were together. Everyone was asking if they ever had a test like this before and we all discussed it.

Each one had a turn. First, a man asked you a bunch of questions. Second, they had a lady put a strap around your stomach and one around your arm. They asked you your name. They wanted you to read something and then they wanted you to repeat it again.

After that, they asked you a series of questions again and again.

It took about a half hour to forty minutes.

They said thank you and you were excused. The partying words were Mr. Stein's usual announcement. No talking about this to anyone!

After that long and stressful day, I had a drink with Barbi. We reflected on our lives, loves and experiences.

I had spent ten years at C&F. The days seemed to melt into one another. I thought about the entire time I had spent in the jewelry business. The people that had danced into my life. I had experienced love and heart-break. Most of all I learned about people.

I was very glad to have spent time with them. Memories good and bad are still memories. All were learning experiences. Some were very bitter pills.

I learned. Hell, I should have been given a PhD.

About a week later, while I was waiting for my paperwork for my new job, I got a message from C&F. They wanted me to come in on a Friday.

I wasn't nervous. I knew I had done nothing wrong. Joe Brickmann had also called me and said he had been asked to take a lie detector test as well.

Joe Brickmann wasn't even there on that day the yellow diamond went missing. I think they wanted to quiz him about the missing Cartier watches.

He was coming in on the same day as I was.

When I arrived most of the people were already inside. I wanted to start singing The Gangs All here but thought better of it.

Mr. Stein waited until everyone was there.

So many looked very nervous. Julie noticed my half smile. In her usual fashion she gave me a shot.

"You are mighty smug, Ms. Nichols."

"No, Julie, I just know I am innocent."

"Really?" She gave me her usual smirk.

No answer from me. I just sat there chanting to myself and looking calm. Why shouldn't I be. Mr. Stein finished with his client. He made his appearance. He started out by saying, "Here are the facts. Two of you failed the test. I'm not going to mention who. I would hope the person or people involved would come forward. That's all I have to say for now. I will be in touch for further tests, and we will uncover the truth. Gia Nichols, kindly remain behind. I would like a few words with you."

I sat there and Julie gave me a parting shot. "Enjoy your day." she said.

After everyone left, Mr. Stein came over to me and sat down.

"Gia, you are cleared of all suspicion. I would just like to say to you, that if you decide to come back here, you would be most welcome. I wish you all the very best in your new position. You will be missed. You will not have to return for any more questions."

As I walked out the door Mr. Peepers and Yori were waiting for me.

"Well, well Nichols, I guess we will be seeing you soon."

"Maybe not." Yori said.

They both started laughing at each other. Mr. Peepers was puffing away on his cigarette. He was smoking nonstop and had been doing this for quite a while.

I wanted to give them a smart remark but thought, say nothing and let them wonder.

The sun was setting. As for me, the pink sky seemed to tell me to put this entire experience behind me and let a new chapter begin.

The End … Or is it?

About the Author

Gia Nichols has worked for over twenty-five years in the diamond industry. She also traveled as a tour operator to many exotic places. She has led many shopping tours, specializing in jewelry, of course.

www.ingramcontent.com/pod-product-compliance
Lightning Source LLC
Chambersburg PA
CBHW030917090426
42737CB00007B/230